SIR ALEX FERGUSON
+ PAUL SCHOLES
"LEGENDS"
THANKS FOR ALL THE
MEMORIES
UNITED
UNITED

MANCHESTER UNITED

Ferguson's Glory Years

Written by
Michael O'Neill

sona
BOOKS

First Published Danann Media Publishing Ltd 2017

Photography courtesy of:
GETTY IMAGES;

Paul Popper/Popperfoto
Manchester Daily Express
Bob Thomas
David Cannon/Allsport
Popperfoto
Russell Cheyne/Allsport
Anton Want/Allsport
Clive Brunskill/Allsport
Ross Kinnaird/Allsport
Matthew Peters / Contributor
Alexander Hassenstein/Bongarts
Shaun Botterill /Allsport
Michael Steele /Allsport
Adrian Dennis/AFP
Manchester United
Tom Purslow/Manchester United
Matthew Peters/Manchester United
Phil Cole
John Peters/Manchester United
Bryn Lennon
Joe Klamar/AFP
Paul Barker/AFP
Paul Ellis/AFP
Alex Livesey
Vladimir Pesnya/Epsilon
liewig christian/Corbis
Dmitry Korotayev/Epsilon
Mark Thompson
AMA/Corbis
Patricia De Melo Moreira/AFP
Laurence Griffiths - The FA
Michael Regan - The FA
Paul Ellis/AFP
Richard Heathcote
Tom Jenkins
Dan Mullan

Book layout & design Darren Grice at Ctrl-d
Copy Editor Tom O'Neill

Made in EU.
CAT NO: SON0493
ISBN: 978-1-912918-55-3

1986 -

Out of the Dark

Ferguson joins Manchester United and stops the rot, but the club still struggles to stay in the top ten. Ferguson experiences his "darkest period" in football. Manchester United's first trophy.

In 1986, Alex Ferguson was forty-four years old and already felt that he'd "... done something worthwhile with his life" by winning the European Cup Winner's Cup as manager of Scottish football club Aberdeen. Fresh from his triumphs, the manager arrived at Old Trafford on the 6th November to try and revive the fortunes of a club that had managed to get no higher than fourth for the previous three consecutive English League Division One seasons. "... to make this club the biggest and best in Europe" was his declared aim. The first years in Manchester proved to be a sobering experience because Lady Success was not to be wooed and won so easily. There was serious work to be done. Both on and off the field. The flotsam and jetsam of the preceding Ron Atkinson era had to be ejected unequivocally along with a lax fitness regime if the biggest club in the world was to regain the longed-for heights of football greatness. There was to be no more "holiday camp" atmosphere. Not under Alexander Chapman Ferguson there wasn't. The manager commented later in life that before coming to Manchester, "I told myself I wasn't going to allow anyone to be stronger than I was. Your personality has to be bigger than theirs. That is vital". The abrupt Scotsman was there to work, five days a week, first in at eight in the morning and last out at night and if he was going to work hard then so was everyone else.

At the time, Manchester was the only club that Ferguson was prepared to leave Aberdeen to manage. *"Taking over a club of the magnitude of Manchester United is an awesome prospect. But ultimately, a football club is a football club and I shall simply try to run things at Old Trafford in what I believe to be the right way", he said in an interview early in his Manchester years. "I am not really interested in what has happened here in the past. I don't mean any disrespect to the great achievements of Manchester United over the years. It's simply that now there is only one way to go, and that is forward. The aim at this club must clearly be to win the championship".*

Fighting words; brave words, because United had won just three games in thirteen when Ferguson arrived. They promptly lost the first game with their new manager in charge, on the 8th November against Oxford United, 2-0. The team was more makeshift than planned with injuries dictating who played and who didn't and Oxford exploited the many problems, surging forward from the start. Even if the Oxford

Alex Ferguson meeting Manchester United fans,
22 November 1986

" Fergie Faces Grim Reality "

player John Aldridge had not been downed and awarded a penalty that put Oxford in front, it probably wouldn't have been long before a goal went in against United.

That first goal came within sixteen minutes of the start. And as Oxford pressed, the beleaguered and sloppy United defence was fortunate to escape further damage. United's attacks were sporadic to say the least, yet despite a weakness in midfield in the Oxford ranks, United were unable to make headway with their loose midfield play either. Even in the second half Oxford gave United no time to sit back as they teased the defence, looking for the second goal. The Red Devils hung on and as the half progressed, it seemed that they might be in with a chance of drawing level; their play became more consistent. Ferguson tried to inject life into the attack rather than rely on defence by putting Jesper Olsen on the field. To no avail. All hopes then vanished in the eightieth minute when the second Oxford goal went in after United failed to clear a cross that hissed in front of their goalmouth.

Ferguson saw the mountain rise up before him. The newspapers writhed with gleeful jibes; *"Fergie Faces Grim Reality" the headlines trumpeted. "Fergie Flops"; "Sad Start for Fergie".*

But they were severely disappointed if they imagined that the new manager would be adversely affected by their diatribes. Sensibly, Ferguson would not be rushed. *"I was born to be a winner", was his reply.*

The rest of the season was a struggle. At times there were angry words from the new boss. Ferguson confessed that his temper was a thing to be feared but he also knew that it could have positive effects and employed it as another management tool, knowing that a player who was 'pinned to the board' once would not be very keen to find himself there for a second time. The players were unceremoniously informed that they were not fit enough. Still, the Scot managed to get his team away from the relegation zone and up to the number eleven spot by season's end. Sighs of relief all around.

But as satisfying as it was to have shot down Liverpool, Arsenal and Manchester City, no one, least of all the manager, was kidding himself about the difficulty of the job in hand. The manager set about reorganising every aspect of the club's activities, altering training regimes and attending to the network of talent scouts and the youth section. He wanted attacking football with forwards confident of strong midfield players behind them, and he wanted a steady flow of new young talent; a dedication to youth that was to pay handsome rewards in the future.

It was fortunate that Ron Atkinson had brought Bryan Robson into the team. Robbo went on to become a legend at Old Trafford, team captain for twelve years and he formed the bedrock of what Ferguson hoped would be a first-class team powerful enough to whack mighty Liverpool off the roof of the football world.

Ferguson had no doubts about what kind of a manager he wanted to be; he was a strong believer in the encouraging effect of the presence of the boss; in the importance of a manager who listened to his player's concerns and above all, in a manager who could instill discipline, the key to success in his eyes. Robbo, unfortunately, was a man who liked his pint so there was potential for conflict. To his credit and the manager's relief, though, Robbo understood and approved of the new message and the brave new world that was within reach if he buckled down. Thanks to Ferguson and his own will power, Robbo was about to achieve a spectacular record and legendary status with the club he loved.

The new man's Scottish temper flared dramatically after a 1-0 defeat to Wimbledon, for the second time, as the season drew to a close. It was reported that he scoured the players for fifteen minutes, roaring at them that he did not expect such performances from United players. This loud blasting seems to

Liverpool goalkeeper Bruce Grobbelaar saves under pressure from Manchester United's Bryan Robson, 15th November 1987

Alex Ferguson (far right) poses with players L-R: Jim Leighton, Mark Hughes, Gordon Strachan and Steve Bruce, August 1988

have had completely the opposite effect to the one intended because the following week, the team was razed to the ground by Tottenham Hotspur, 4-0. The penultimate match against Coventry City couldn't have done much to abate the manager's ire, either, with a 1-1 result, and winning 3-1 in the last game of the season against Aston Villa in front of a home crowd was insufficient to save the Manchester careers of some of the players.

No doubt one of the greatest pleasures for Ferguson during that season was knowing that United had beaten Liverpool 1-0 on two occasions. Liverpool; the manager's personal bête noire; the Liverpool that the Manchester United man had sworn to knock off their perch.

Ferguson had said he would wait out the season before buying new players, and now that he had seen the full extent of the job in hand he set to work. He wasn't sentimental. Reputations, he asserted, were nothing to him. Whoever they were and however big they were, if he was not impressed with

" I'll not let the disappointment of this season dishearten me "

players' performances they would be on their way, a credo he was to adhere to and follow many times in future years to the dismay of many. The axe fell; Frank Stapleton and Terry Gibson were given their marching orders.

Jim Leighton, Viv Anderson, Brian McClair – who proved to be a godsend, scoring thirty-one goals in total that season – and Steve Bruce, brought new blood and vigour into the team, and the effects were immediate.

After an uncertain start to the new season of 1987-88, the results began to run in United's favour and suddenly it seemed as if a miracle might have occurred. Ferguson's love of attacking football was paying off, so it appeared; United went on to lose only five games. They drew twelve, however, and that scuppered their chances of the title. Two of those draws were against the leaders of the axis of evil, in Ferguson's eyes, Liverpool. Although United won eight of the last ten games, they came in second behind Liverpool; their rivals had 90 points and they had 81. There had been an extraordinary match away against the Merseyside team in April 1988 that had seen United pull back from 3-1 to end the game level, so spirits were high at this abrupt change in fortune.

The match at Liverpool was a cracker with Manchester proving that they were not afraid of the big boys when they took the lead after just two minutes, and it was the great Bryan Robson who struck that first goal after United had ravaged the Liverpool defence. Stung into action by such impudence, United were left reeling by a Liverpool side out for revenge, and at times, it seemed as though only the tenacious Irishman Paul McGrath, widely thought to be one of the best Irish players ever, stood between United and destruction. It was obvious that United could not hold out forever, and thirty minutes into the game Liverpool had drawn level. Now they went forward again and with four minutes left before the half-time whistle, the Merseyside team got their reward, their second goal.

Ferguson didn't need to be a genius to realise, once the game had restarted, that unless he came up with a dramatic change, the points were going to Liverpool, because United had conceded another goal less than a minute after the whistle sounded. In the fifty-fourth minute, he sent on Norman Whiteside and Jesper Olsen. The tide slowly began to turn when in the sixty-fifth minute, Robson let rip from eighteen yards. It was now 3-2, and Liverpool had to contend with the Manchester waves crashing against their defences. In a rare moment of paralysis, they allowed gaps to be filled with Manchester players and the equaliser then came from the foot of Strachan. It was a fighting comeback that the fans would learn that they could expect many times in the future. Nonetheless, the match left the manager angry, rightly or wrongly, and he suggested that Liverpool's elevated status was responsible for intimidating referees into making decisions unfavourable to visiting teams. But if so, what goes around comes around, as Ferguson would discover.

It was a lesser consideration for the fans, who were just happy that after so many years their club seemed to be back in contention for the trophies.

And then the bubble burst.

The words Ferguson uttered in April 1989, *"I'll not let the disappointment of this season dishearten me"*, sum up the results of that year. The league table spoke volumes. Arsenal won the title with 76 points. United came in eleventh with 51.

Division 1, Manchester United's Mark Hughes and Liverpool's Gary Gillespie battle for the ball, September 1990

" what I have felt in the last week you wouldn't think should happen in football "

There had been booing from the terraces, perhaps the most unwelcome sound to a manager's ears and often the doom-laden heralds of terminating contracts. Unsurprising, though, after just three wins in the fourteen games from the middle of February 1989 until the end of the season in May. Empty seats told their own story. Unthinkable to imagine what might have happened if the directors had lost their nerve. They held steady.

Stretford End favourites Norman Whiteside and Paul McGrath were let go as Ferguson cleared the dressing room of this generation of the old style of players. Eighteen players had now left the club since Ferguson's appointment; sixteen had arrived. In the light of the results, not everyone approved of the upheaval.

For the new season of 1989/90, Ferguson tried to bolster the side by bringing in Danny Wallace, Mike Phelan, Neil Webb and Paul Ince at considerable cost. They only seemed to add fuel to the funeral pyre. After a 4-1 win against Arsenal for the first game of the season, the side lost their grip completely, taking in three defeats in the next four games. Hope flared momentarily with a 5-1 home win against Millwall on the 16th of September 1989, only to have its legs chopped viciously away from it in the match on the 23rd of September against Manchester City, which represented the humiliating nadir of United's season. The best that could be salvaged was a maxim: every cloud has a silver lining; after all, it couldn't get any worse.

That match had delivered a painful mauling, however, and the pain had begun almost straightaway. Just eleven minutes in and City's David Oldfield pounced on a cross that Pallister had failed to clear, making it 1-0. Barely did United have time to recover before the second goal went in following a shambles by the defence in front of their own goal. And then a beautiful flowing move took City from their own half right down in front of the United goal where an Ian Bishop header put a floundering United three behind.

But never giving up, United were put back in the game with a brilliant bicycle kick by Mark Hughes from the floating cross sent over by Beardsmore, who had set himself up for a cross-goal strike by skillfully evading the City defence. It was just a brief moment of hope, because before long, City had split United's defence once more for David Oldfield to slot his second into an empty goalmouth. Adding insult to injury, Andy Hinchcliffe was there to receive the ball on his head and powerfully hit number five after another swift, defence-splitting, flowing movement by City. Low points did not get much lower than this.

Ferguson felt the club's pain personally, and it was compounded by the fact that they had been waiting twenty-two years for the championship. *"Believe me", said Ferguson after the defeat, "what I have felt in the last week you wouldn't think should happen in football".* Despite it all, he was convinced that he had done the right thing in convincing the club to go into the red for new players. Yet nothing seemed to do the trick.

Ferguson knew that despite the board's understanding of his difficulties with injuries, if the season continued in the same way, then he would probably no longer be manager in the summer. Rumours abounded that several senior figures at the club were expressing their dissatisfaction with the manager.

Everyone and their dog, it seemed, was bashing the club and Ferguson, and calls for him to go blared out from the press and the terraces. The Scot could not make the team gel and the brickbats came thick and fast. *"Fergie's last stand", "The worst record of any United manager of modern times", roared the headlines. Mocking banners appeared stating; "Three years of excuses and it's still crap... ta-ra Fergie".* It was relentless.

Ferguson admitted later that this was the *"darkest period"* that he had ever suffered in his entire football career.

After a goalless draw against Sheffield Wednesday in October in front of a home crowd, the players were booed off the pitch.

Following a moment of recovery when they lost just one game and won four - four games that undoubtedly helped to save Alex Ferguson's neck - they then entered an eleven-game run without a win, ushered in with a 0-0 draw against Chelsea in November, which stretched out interminably into February 1990. Fans had to endure the sight of their team drooping in game after game, losing 1-0 to Arsenal, 2-1 to Crystal Palace and 1-0 to Tottenham Hotspur. Fortunately,

Legendary former Manchester United Manager Sir Matt Busby (right) meets with the current United Manager, Old Trafford, 1991

they just about saved face against both Liverpool, 0-0, and at home against Manchester City, 1-1. But at least the drought ended with that match and a 2-1 defeat of Millwall brought them back from the dead.

They dropped to seventeenth in the table and continued to stutter on until the middle of May when four wins hauled them back up to thirteenth only for two more losses and a draw to drop them back to sixteenth. Pallister saved their blushes in the final match of the season at home against Charlton Athletic in a 1-0 win.

Try as he may, Ferguson could not get the team away from 15th or 16th until that blessed 1-0 win against Charlton Athletic took them to 13th place.

And yet.

Something astonishing was about to happen. And the effect was so enormous it altered the club's history.

United had thrashed their way through to the FA Cup Final having only just beaten Newcastle United, 3-2, and Sheffield United, 1-0, and surviving a semi-final replay against Oldham, which they won 2-1 after extra time. They found themselves facing yet another replay in the final following a 3-3 draw against Crystal Palace.

Ferguson thought long and hard about what to do to salvage the dream of the trophy. For the replay, he decided to replace goalkeeper Jim Leighton, angering a great many people in doing so. When it was announced that Les Sealey, on loan from Luton Town, would be his replacement it was difficult not to overhear the boos floating up from the crowd.

"I knew I was right", Ferguson commented later.

And he was.

"Ugly and illegitimate assaults", as one reporter put it, marred the game. Crystal Palace had decided that they would crush United physically if nothing else, and attacked. Predictably, the football was scrappy and unproductive, and unwarranted attacks paired with bad temper made for a match unworthy of final. Almost twenty-five minutes passed in this unsatisfactory manner until Palace decided to actually play football. With Manchester under pressure, Sealey proved that the manager's faith in him had not been misplaced. United were fortunate to escape a penalty against them during a bad-tempered fray in front of goal, but as the first half drew to a close, the Red Devils began to settle and recover some of their momentum. By the time the second half got under way, the team had calmed even though the game continued to be ruined by unnecessary physical attacks on both sides.

Nonetheless, it was United who kept their heads, and with a superbly accurate pass, Webb the floated the ball to Martin, who brought it under control before rifling a shot into the top of the Palace net. Once again, Sealey kept the ball out of the net, during a goalmouth melee this time, and with neither team managing to convert their other chances into goals, the cup was finally held aloft by the United team. That last goal meant a seventh FA Cup trophy for the team, but one unimaginably mighty step for the club. Perhaps understandably, the manager, who had been under such intense pressure all season and perhaps in this game in particular, had little to say except to praise both Les Sealey and goalscorer Lee Martin.

That Lee Martin goal saved Alex Ferguson's career at Manchester, because if United had lost that game, faith in him would have ebbed away and it would have been impossible to keep the baying hounds tied up for much longer.

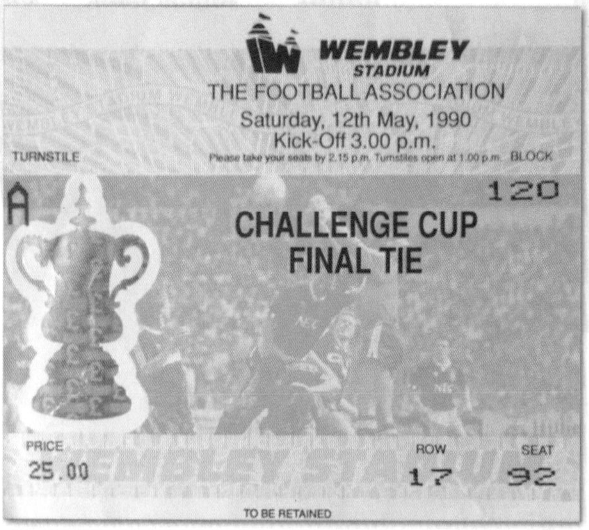
WEMBLEY
STADIUM
THE FOOTBALL ASSOCIATION
Saturday, 12th May, 1990
Kick-Off 3.00 p.m.
Please take your seats by 2.15 p.m. Turnstiles open at 1.00 p.m.
TURNSTILE
A
BLOCK
120
CHALLENGE CUP
FINAL TIE
PRICE
25.00
ROW
17
SEAT
92
TO BE RETAINED

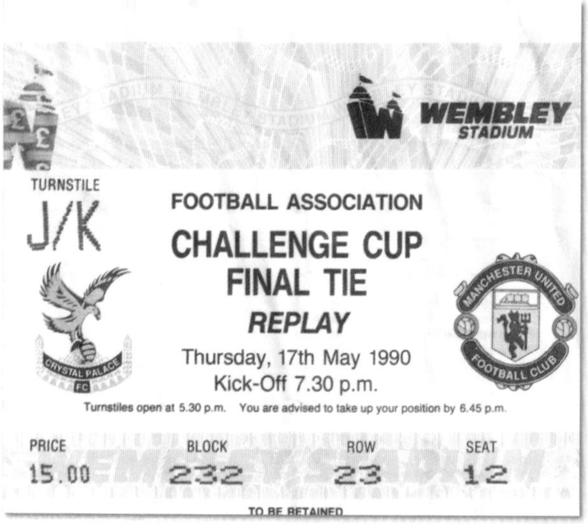
WEMBLEY
STADIUM
TURNSTILE
J/K
FOOTBALL ASSOCIATION
CHALLENGE CUP
FINAL TIE
REPLAY
Thursday, 17th May 1990
Kick-Off 7.30 p.m.
Turnstiles open at 5.30 p.m. You are advised to take up your position by 6.45 p.m.
PRICE
15.00
BLOCK
232
ROW
23
SEAT
12
TO BE RETAINED

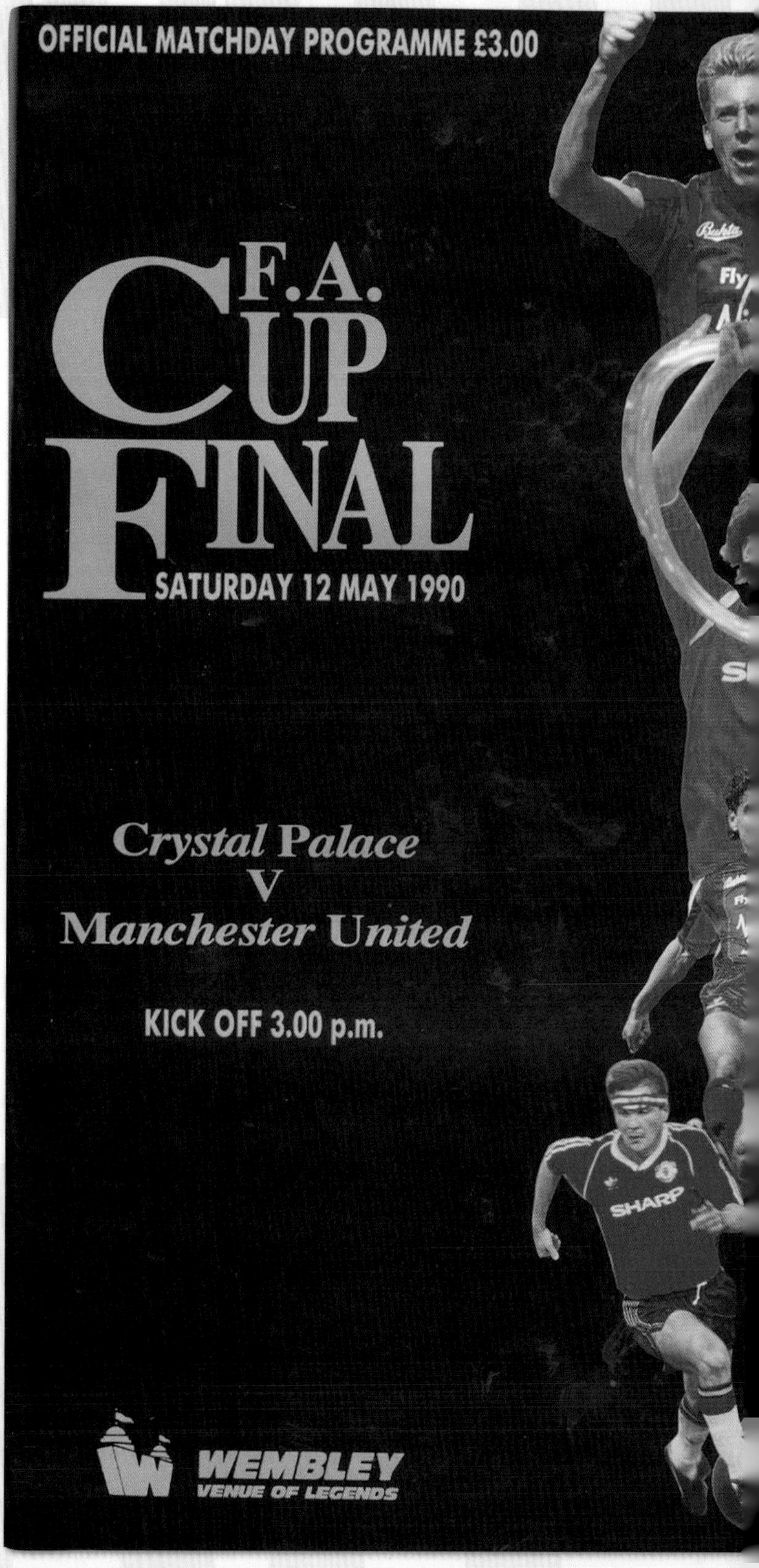
OFFICIAL MATCHDAY PROGRAMME £3.00
F.A. CUP FINAL
SATURDAY 12 MAY 1990
Crystal Palace
V
Manchester United
KICK OFF 3.00 p.m.
WEMBLEY
VENUE OF LEGENDS

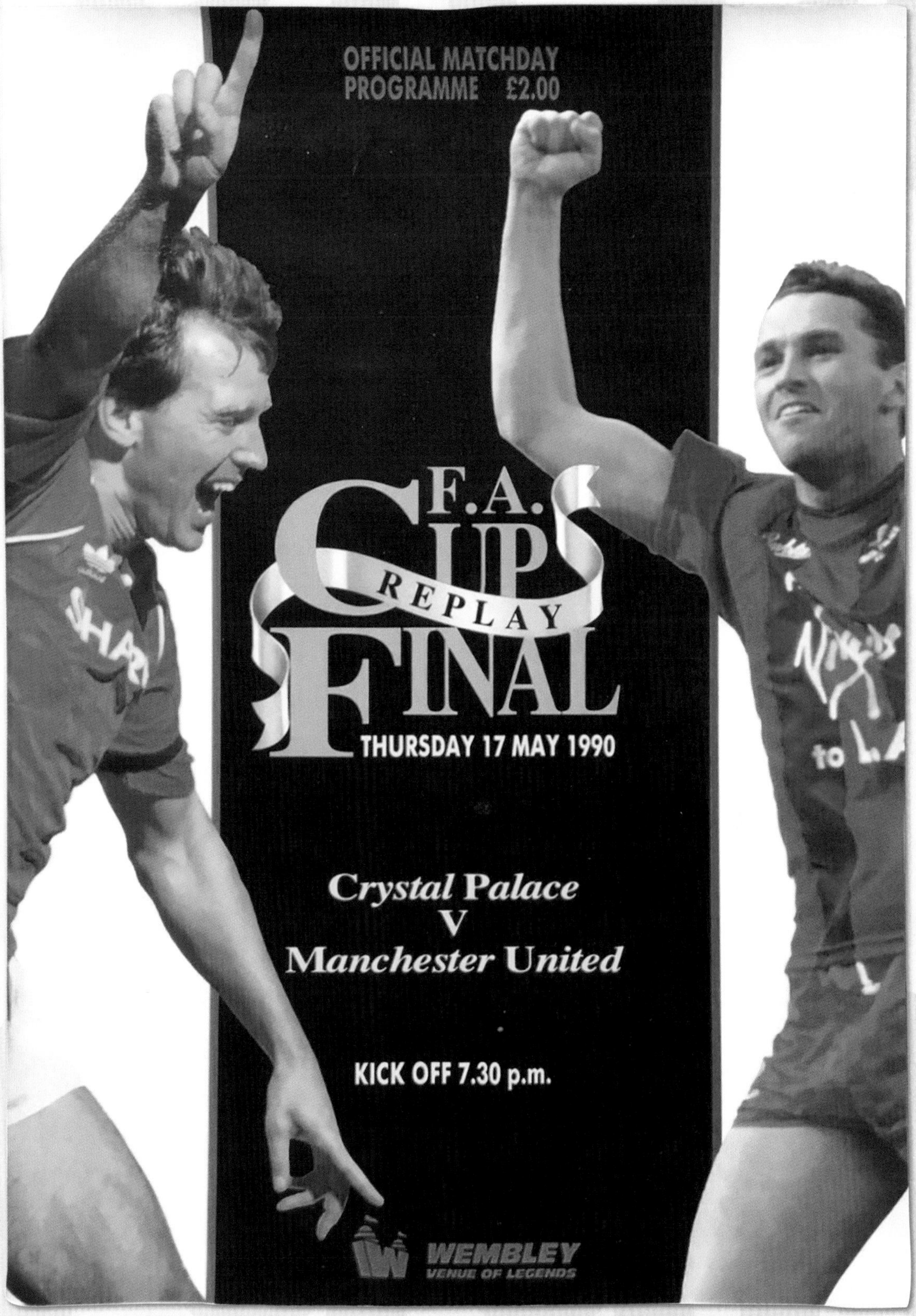
OFFICIAL MATCHDAY
PROGRAMME £2.00
F.A. CUP
REPLAY
FINAL
THURSDAY 17 MAY 1990
Crystal Palace
V
Manchester United
KICK OFF 7.30 p.m.
WEMBLEY
VENUE OF LEGENDS

1990 - Into the light

Eric Cantona arrives and United begin to shine. Ferguson is first Premier League Manager of the Month. The League and Cup Double.

"OK, you've proved you can win the FA Cup, now go back to Scotland".

Alex Ferguson never forgot that bitter headline that greeted his and United's FA Cup win in 1990. It was ugly, the press at its worst. But Ferguson was not about to give in to the rabble-rousers.

"I know that I am doing the job the right way and the motivation of the players is no problem", he had said. He would finish the job but he would finish it his way.

United's young players were always in the crosshairs of his attention and that is how it would remain, and the boys repaid the boss's loyalty in them by heaving the team into 6th position in the 1990/91 season.

There had been several stinging defeats; losing 0-2 to Everton at home had doubtless been one of them; losing 0-1 at home to Nottingham Forest wasn't much fun either. Losing to Chelsea twice by the same scoreline 2-3, was doubtless guaranteed to send the manager's temper skywards, as well. The worst of them all, however, took place in the match against Liverpool on the 16th of September 1990.

Yet initially in that game, as United pressed forward stretching Grobbelaar in the Liverpool goal, it seemed as though all was well. It was Beardsley, who put paid to that impression when Liverpool razed open United's defence and the Manchester side were suddenly one down. Just eleven minutes had passed. United were determined not to be has-beens so soon, and almost equalised; but the ball bounced off the bar. Encouraged, United pressed forward with incisive football, prevented only from success by the swift hands of Grobbelaar. Liverpool, lethally dangerous when in front of goal, scythed open the United defence again and went two up when another swift move gave Beardsley his second. And because Liverpool seemed to want the ball more than United they were rewarded with a third goal; Barnes this time. The difference between the two teams could be seen when Webb came so close, but United lacked the biting finish in front of goal when it mattered.

In contrast, Liverpool were on a high, passing the ball swiftly and accurately and could have scored several more at this point launching some exciting attacks as they piled towards the United goal. United's attacks both lacked creativity and faltered at crucial moments. And then Beardsley

1994

SHARP
SHARP
4

LEFT: 1990 FA Cup Final, Wembley, Manchester United 3 v Crystal Palace 3, Mark Hughes celebrates scoring his first goal with Brian McClair, 12th May 1990

ABOVE: 1990 FA Cup Final Replay, Wembley, Manchester United 1 v Crystal Palace 0, captain Bryan Robson outjumps Crystal Palace's Alan Pardew, 17th May 1990

Mark Hughes celebrates with the trophy as Steve Bruce looks on after the 1991 European Cup Winners Cup Final against Barcelona, 15th May 1991 in Rotterdam, Holland.

" ... gives you stature and it gives you a presence "

put in the knife with a fourth goal lobbed over the head of Sealey after a rapidly taken free kick.

Revenge soon came to soothe injured pride; Liverpool were dumped out of the League Cup in the third round in October when United pushed them out 3-1. A quite satisfactory result in everyone's eyes. With the bit between their teeth they then laid into Arsenal in the next round and crushed them 6-2. On a roll, United made their way through to the final against Sheffield Wednesday in April.

When their luck ran out.

It was close; 1-0. But the runner up isn't remembered; you might as well have not played.

So, sixth in the League it was, still far off the top, though. With 53 points to Arsenal's 89, Ferguson was acutely aware that there was an awful lot still to do before that league title that everyone wanted popped up in front of them. Twenty-three years had passed since United had last won the League. It was a wound in United's side that required urgent attention. Fergie had a little surprise tidbit to offer the fans to keep them happy during the wait, though.

The European competitions were now open to British clubs again, after the Heysel Stadium disaster of 1985 had seen them banned for five years. United entered the Cup Winner's Cup competition and had gone through all the stages fairly smoothly to set up a glamorous final against Barcelona. Barcelona were one of Europe's big fish and for United, this was a first taste of what glamour looked like, the glamour that they so craved.

On a rain-soaked night, Ferguson had made another of his courageous decisions; this time to replace Neil Webb with Mike Phelan. And once more, the canny Scot proved that he knew his football. From a cautious start, United began to take the game towards the Spaniards and were unlucky with several attempts at goal. In fact, Les Sealey made his first save of the night just two minutes before half-time, and even then the ball was fired straight at him. United had the best of the play, their confidence growing whilst their opponents seemed to lack ideas. The English team, however, had still been unable to truly test their opposition's defences.

United began the second half with lively play and fought their way through to within firing range of the Spanish goal, but with ragged teamwork they were unable to convert any of the moves into goals. Soon, their confidence too began to ebb; bringing danger and caution found its way back into the game. Sixty-eight minutes had now passed. This stalemate was not good.

Then United were awarded a free kick and Robson's floating ball swerved away from the keeper leaving him in two minds about what to do. Bruce connected with the ball in the air and headed it past the keeper towards the goal where Hughes helped it over the line. The game was blown wide open and United had the advantage. It didn't take five minutes for Manchester to cement their lead when Robson again found Hughes, who took the ball past the advancing Spanish goalkeeper and drove it into the net for his and Manchester's second goal. Ferguson was watching his groundwork for the long term translate into results.

And then; a dreadful moment when Koeman's free kick got the better of Les Sealey; 2-1 in the seventy-ninth minute. United had to fight for their lives. Hughes almost claimed a third but was taken down in a foul that earned a red card. In the end it didn't matter. With those two goals from Hughes, the plaudits and another trophy were winging their way back to Manchester. 2-1 to United. Ferguson's plan for United was beginning to bear fruit.

He was pleased for another reason; Ferguson was convinced that success brought another benefit. Success *"... gives you stature and it gives you a presence", he said. "When*

Rumbelows League Cup Final, Wembley, Manchester United 1 v Nottingham Forest 0, Manchester United captain Steve Bruce holds the trophy aloft, 12th April 1992

"... beat the best and lose to the worst"

Liverpool were at their peak they won games simply because they were Liverpool and teams feared them. Their name won them games". Ferguson knew that this cup was another important step to arriving at those glorious heights of fame.

Whilst Ferguson knew the team was playing well, he also knew they needed a little oil before they could really start speeding along. He brought the young Ryan Giggs into the first team permanently – he won the PFA Young Player of the Year award in 1992 and 1993 – and strengthened the defences by buying *"... the bargain of the century"*, as Ferguson described it, Danish keeper Peter Schmeichel. Schmeichel was the World's Best Goalkeeper in 1992 and 1993, proving that Fergie knew a bargain when he saw one.

And now the team truly did begin to fire on all cylinders. Here, after patiently building his side and believing in himself, after agonising years of waiting, Ferguson had a team for the fans to be proud of. His boys were championship material; of that he was certain. Yes, they were guilty of inconsistence, too; they could *"... beat the best and lose to the worst", as he put it. Still, confidence was breaking out all over and Ferguson was in the vanguard: "I can't say we will win the League next season but I certainly hope we will be up there alongside Liverpool".*

An historic season was upon them as United powered their way through the table in 1991/92, starting with twelve games without defeat and bouncing between 1st and 2nd place in the table. Luton town disappeared under a five-goal onslaught in September, and in December, Coventry were lashed with four goals, 4-0, and there was a six-goal feast for the fans to savour in a 6-3 away win against Oldham Athletic. The Red Devils were not quite so surefooted for the rest of the season which saw them involved in ten drawn games that very effectively deprived them of the title.

A stutter at the final hurdle, losing three of the last four games, one of them, irritatingly, against Liverpool, 2-0, saw the title go to Leeds United by a margin of four points, 78 to 82.

There had been one awful game to endure. It had taken place on the 1st of January 1992 against Queens Park Rangers in front of a home crowd. Queens Park Rangers ended the season in the middle of the table; they shouldn't have been a problem. But they were. The game was, in fact, one enormous nightmare in which United played the role of Judy to Rangers' Mr. Punch. The result of United acting as though the game hadn't started at all, was that Rangers had the ball in the back of the net after just three minutes. That still didn't wake them up; Manchester fans were punished again two minutes later when their team found themselves 2-0 down.

The agony was only just beginning, because the Londoners kept rattling at the United defence, stretching it thin so that the home side were left chasing the game, constantly on the wrong foot. The sorry statistic of half-time was that United had not had one single shot at goal. Predictably, this brought forth a shower of boos from the crowd.

The second half, despite the manager's half-time talk, failed to ignite United's game and they were only briefly more involved than in the first half. Rangers were soon back in the driving seat and it seemed like only a question of time before the next goal came. Which it duly did in the fifty-eighth minute with Schmeichel beaten again via a lob this time to make it three to the visitors.

It was a minor miracle then that with just eight minutes left to go, McClair managed to grab one back for United. Perhaps the team might have found more incentive to play if an earlier attempt by McClair, when he had put the ball into the goal for the first time, had not been disallowed. But the game was already over, so that when Bailey hit Rangers' fourth and the Londoners almost grabbed a fifth, none of the Manchester crowd really cared any more.

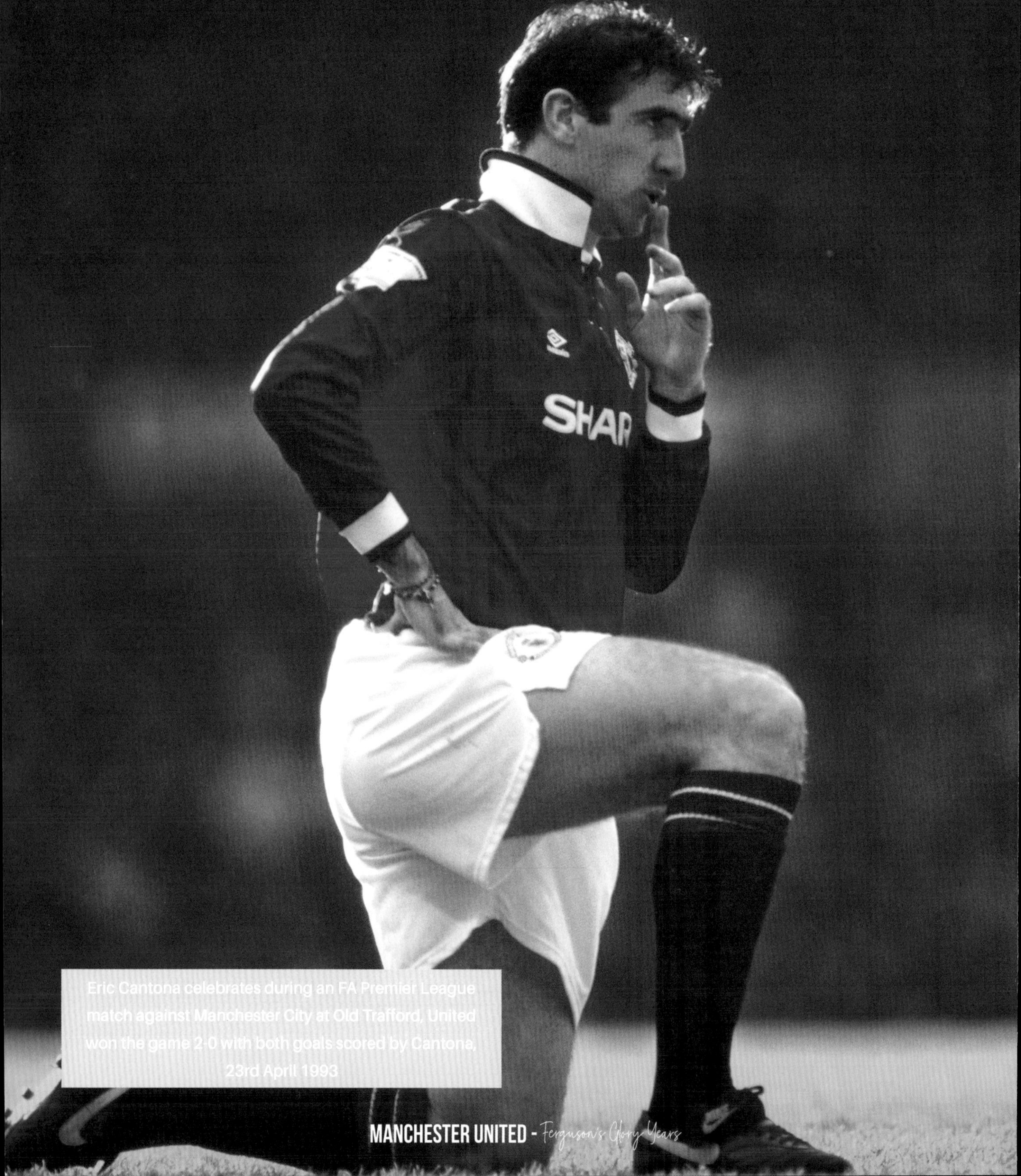

Eric Cantona celebrates during an FA Premier League match against Manchester City at Old Trafford, United won the game 2-0 with both goals scored by Cantona, 23rd April 1993

" … walking in as though he owned the bloody place "

The lacklustre performance by his club caused the manager to exclaim that it was *"unbelievable"*. His team, he confessed, had been totally outplayed and he neither had nor was he about to make any excuses whatsoever. The best he could hope for was that it was a one-off and that having had a rest, the team would now fight for the rest of the season. They did, but just weren't quite good enough for that league title. Lack of goals had been United's Achilles' heel that season but nothing had come of Fergie's attempts at finding a good striker.

However, as the fans had now come to expect, almost, Fergie had a pretty shiny consolation prize up his sleeve. The League Cup, won on the 12th of April 1-0 against Nottingham Forest; it was the first time the club had won the trophy. Not enough for the moaners, it seemed. It was the League or nothing; not enough for Ferguson, either, as he was disappointed, too. *"I was born to be a winner"* he is quoted as saying. By which he obviously meant a winner in the League or in Europe.

The old English League Division One was now no longer the top league. It had been superseded by the new Premier League for the start of the 1992/93 season, and the start into the new world was not auspicious for United. Twenty-six years had passed by without a league title. Ferguson needed another firecracker in the team. Someone to inspire and ignite the spirit of success.

He found the firecracker at league champions Leeds United.

Now and again, in all walks of life, two people find each other in the crowd, the sparks crackle, and energy and creativity are released in ways that would not otherwise have been possible had they never met. In music, McCartney and Lennon, of course. In the world of football, one of those rare relationships was about to catapult the Manchester United club into superstardom. A player came to United and turned it upside down, a man who would ever after bear the epithet King Eric: Frenchman Eric Cantona.

Together, he and Ferguson would form a winning team without parallel at the club. The canny Ferguson recognised the extraordinary talent and knew how it needed to be treated; he offered friendship, gave it room to breathe, showered it with nourishment and justified respect, and left the whip and lash for others to wield. Ferguson and United lavished love on the Frenchman and he blossomed and repaid them tenfold. As Bobby Charlton said of him, *"A player like that only comes along once or twice in a lifetime"*.

To Ferguson's delight, he had come, *"… walking in as though he owned the bloody place"*, and United were about to set the world alight.

Cantona's first competitive match was on the 6th December 1992 and before the end of the month he had scored three goals. The team that had been fifth now began to remove the opposition on its way to the top.

In March after a 2-1 win against Liverpool, admittedly not the team they had once been, United were on the top spot. The smell of success was in the air. And then came an unexpected defeat at the hands of Oldham Athletic on the 9th of March, 0-1, followed by three draws, one, fatally, against title rivals Aston Villa at home 1-1. When they came to play Sheffield Wednesday on the 10th of April 1993, they had dropped into second place, one point behind Aston Villa. There would then be just five games left to see off the bogeyman and take the title. So the match was a vital stepping stone that really needed to be won by the Manchester side.

Sheffield Wednesday were not to be underestimated, even though fifteen points separated the two teams. But their two top strikers, David Hirst and Paul Warhurst, (twelve goals in twelve games) were absent so it seemed that a defensive game by Sheffield Wednesday might allow United to perform their magic upfront.

Not so, and although United had their chances, the goals failed to materialise and Sheffield Wednesday had a dangerous man up front, Chris Waddle, so the half-time score of 0-0 was unsatisfactory to say the least.

As the second half got underway, Michael Peck, the referee, had to leave the field with a leg injury and a new referee took over; John Hilditch. He was barely on the field before Wednesday launched another attack and with Waddle in the penalty area it produced a dangerous moment. Ince ended it by whipping the legs away from a Wednesday player. Without hesitation, the new referee awarded a penalty. Sheridan stepped up. He struck the ball to Schmeichel's right with the goalkeeper moving in the opposite direction. Suddenly United needed to pay serious attention and bring sharpness into the game.

Ferguson brought on Bryan Robson to replace Paul Parker. His team was displaying some sparkling moments; one of them when brisk passing resulted in Hughes getting through for a shot, only to be denied by swift reactions from Chris Woods in the Wednesday goal. United were now focusing on the Wednesday goal, at least, to produce any effective finishing.

Twelve minutes to go and United were awarded a corner. In a do or die effort to at least salvage a point, everyone went into the Wednesday half. As the cross looped out towards the outside of the penalty area, Bruce rose to meet it, and a superbly judged gunshot header had the ball in the back of the

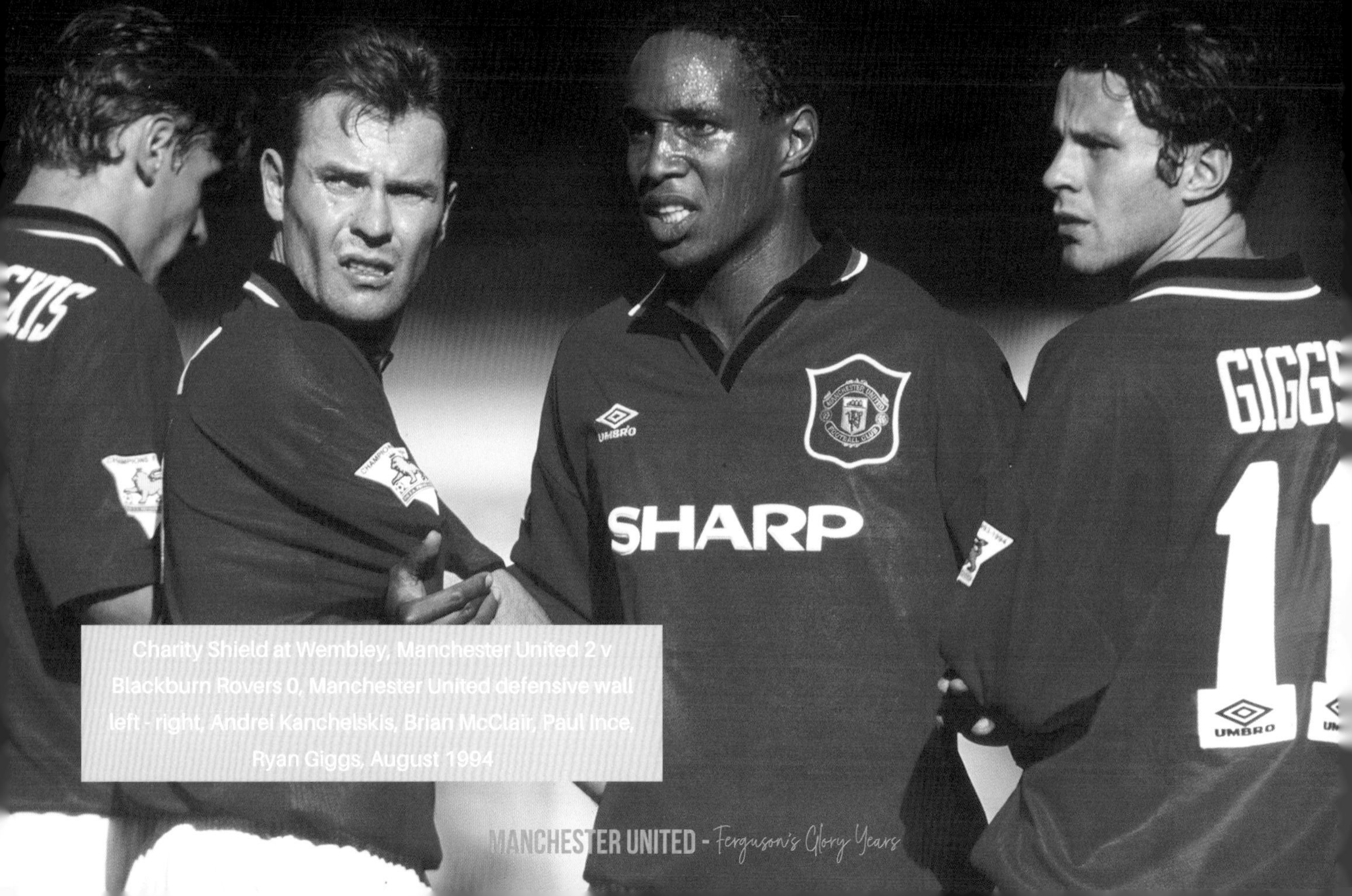

Charity Shield at Wembley, Manchester United 2 v Blackburn Rovers 0, Manchester United defensive wall left - right, Andrei Kanchelskis, Brian McClair, Paul Ince, Ryan Giggs, August 1994

net. The roar might have been heard in Scotland. United were back with a chance of the title.

Not content with a draw, United began to pile on the pressure. Ninety minutes had come and gone, six minutes of injury time had been added on and still the referee did not blow the whistle. United came forward again. Wednesday blunted the attack but failed to capitalise on their advantage and Pallister picked up the ball on the right sending it back into Wednesday's danger zone. Once again Wednesday failed to clear it, and the ball looped into the air where Bruce was lurking. He picked his spot and placed the header wide of the flailing Wednesday keeper.

It had taken United far too long and without the injury time they would have failed. It was fortunate, too, for the struggling Manchester side, that Wednesday had been without their top strikers. But results count and it was now 2-1.

Even Ferguson, stoic throughout, couldn't prevent his excitement from showing. As he rushed to the touchline, he leapt into the air fists stretched skywards. Brian Kidd couldn't contain himself, either, and leaped onto the pitch where he fell to his knees in disbelief. The three points gave United the number one spot again. And there they stayed winning the final five games, which included a wonderful 3-0 victory over Chelsea and a 3-1 victory over Blackburn Rovers. Both games in front of ecstatic home crowds.

At last, the league title was theirs again. No matter that all cup challenges had spluttered and gone out. Ferguson had given the fans what they wanted. In guiding and moulding his team, resolute amongst all the stresses and strains, Ferguson had never shown more understanding of human nature than he had with his star Eric Cantona; he had needed all his psychological skills and knowledge to keep Cantona even vaguely inside the permissible standards of behaviour. But it had paid off in a shower of gold.

Well, silver, but who cared?

For that 1993/94 season, Ferguson had lined up what was considered to be the finest squad in England. In Ryan Giggs, Mark Hughes and Eric Cantona, Ferguson had moulded a formidable attacking trio. Giggs had joined United on his fourteenth birthday and went on to become the most decorated player in football history. Before he left the club, he would win thirteen Premier League winners' medals, three League Cup winners' medals, four FA Cup winners' medals, and two Champions League winners' medals just to mention a part of his haul.

Mark Hughes would boast Barcelona, Bayern Munich and Chelsea on his CV in later years, two Premier League title medals, four FA Cups, three League Cups, and two European Cup Winners' Cup's. Partnered with Eric Cantona, they became a close-knit pair whose cooperation went from strength to strength. What a front row! What a turn around! And what a season! United powered by Cantona and his twenty-five goals had been on top of the League table for all but two of the matches. They had swept away the opposition to take the title with 92 points, 8 clear of Blackburn Rovers. Six days later they had wiped out Chelsea, 4-0, in the FA Cup final, becoming just the fourth club in the 20th century to win the Double.

Ferguson's eye for talent was working supremely well and his philosophy of the game was paying off big time. He had proven to others what he already knew; that as a manager he had the talent to bring home the silver. Had he not been given the first Premier League Manager of the Month award for August 1993?

What he was about to prove in the 1994/95 season, however, was that he possessed characteristics of equally crucial value in forming a trophy-winning team; understanding, loyalty, respect and the steadfastness and strength to follow where they led him.

SHARP
Candy
SHARP
TENNENT'S
F.A. CHARITY SHIELD
Liverpool v Manchester United
SATURDAY 18th AUGUST 1990
KICK-OFF 3.00pm
OFFICIAL MATCHDAY PROGRAMME £2.50

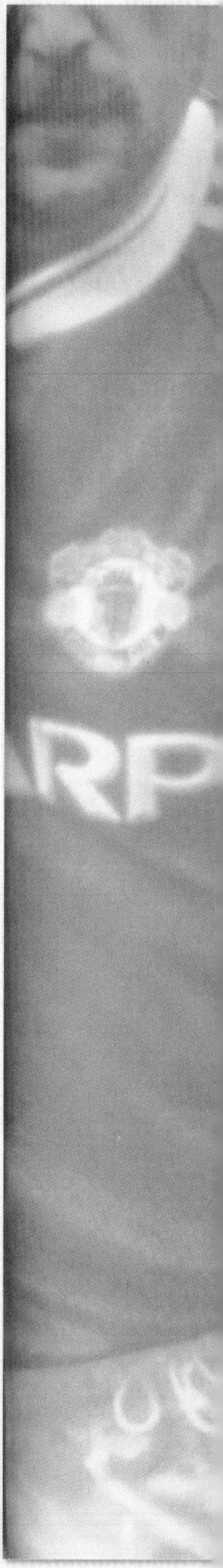

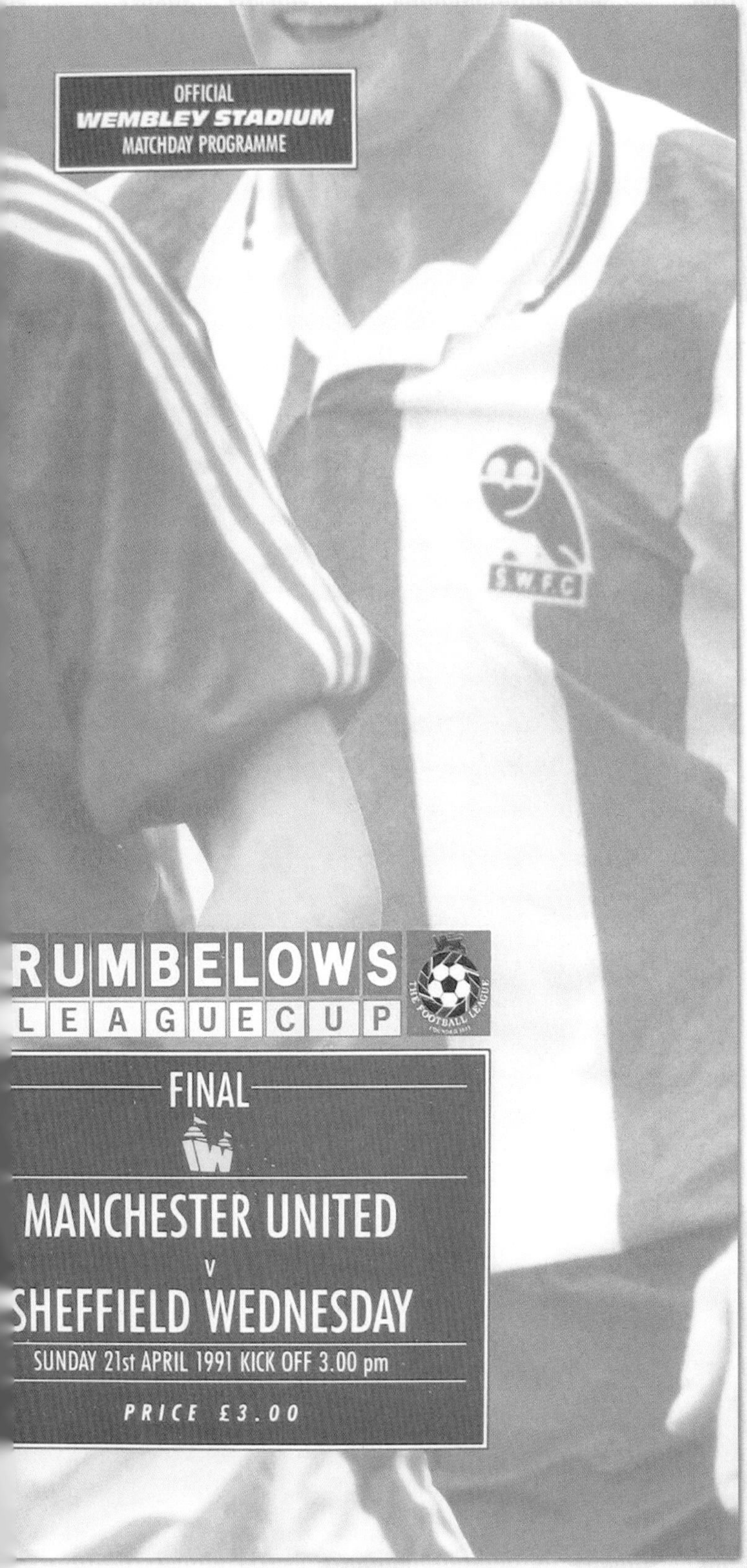
OFFICIAL
WEMBLEY STADIUM
MATCHDAY PROGRAMME
S.W.F.C.
RUMBELOWS
LEAGUE CUP
THE FOOTBALL LEAGUE
FINAL
MANCHESTER UNITED
v
SHEFFIELD WEDNESDAY
SUNDAY 21st APRIL 1991 KICK OFF 3.00 pm
PRICE £3.00

WEMBLEY STADIUM
Gates open 1.00 p.m.
You are advised to take up your position by 2.30 p.m.
TENNENT'S
F.A. CHARITY SHIELD
Saturday
18th August 1990
Kick-Off 3.00 p.m.
BLOCK
TURNSTILE
H
238
MANCHESTER UNITED FOOTBALL CLUB
LIVERPOOL FOOTBALL CLUB
PRICE
18.00
ROW
7
SEAT
11
WEMBLEY STADIUM
TO BE RETAINED

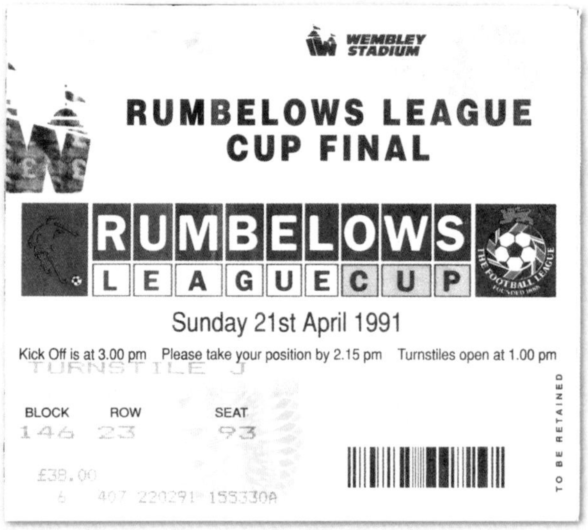
WEMBLEY STADIUM
RUMBELOWS LEAGUE
CUP FINAL
RUMBELOWS
LEAGUE CUP
THE FOOTBALL LEAGUE
Sunday 21st April 1991
Kick Off is at 3.00 pm
Please take your position by 2.15 pm
Turnstiles open at 1.00 pm
TURNSTILE J
BLOCK
146
ROW
23
SEAT
93
£38.00
6 407 220291 155330A
TO BE RETAINED

RUMBELOWS
LEAGUE CUP
THE FOOTBALL LEAGUE
FINAL
MANCHESTER UNITED
V
NOTTINGHAM FOREST
SUNDAY APRIL 12 1992
KICK-OFF 3.00PM
WEMBLEY
STADIUM LIMITED
OFFICIAL MATCHDAY PROGRAMME £3.00

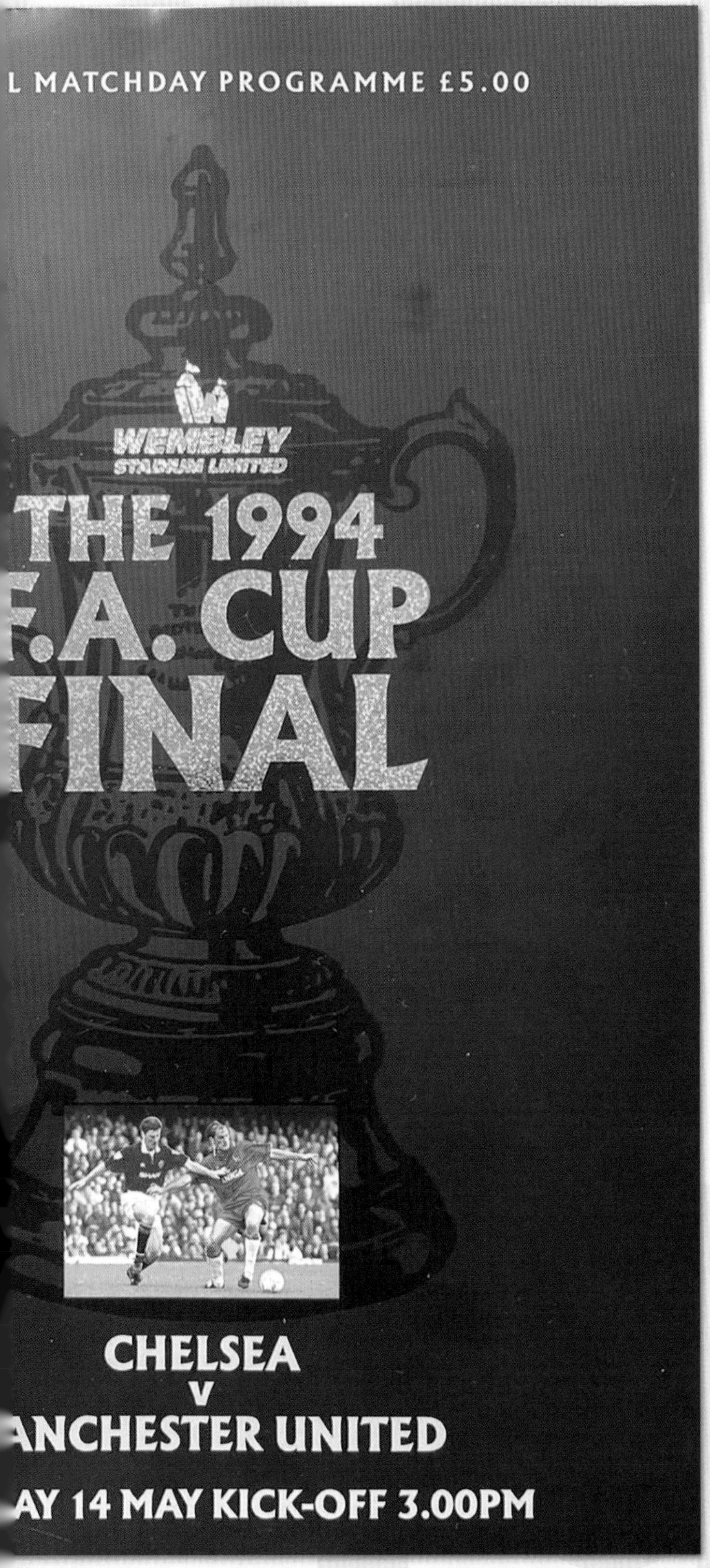
L MATCHDAY PROGRAMME £5.00
WEMBLEY STADIUM LIMITED
THE 1994
F.A. CUP
FINAL
CHELSEA
V
ANCHESTER UNITED
AY 14 MAY KICK-OFF 3.00PM

WEMBLEY STADIUM
RUMBELOWS
LEAGUE CUP
SUNDAY 12TH APRIL 1992
KICK-OFF IS AT 3.00 PM
PLEASE TAKE YOUR POSITION BY 2.15 PM
TURNSTILES OPEN AT 1.00 PM
TURNSTILE M
BLOCK ROW SEAT
228 16 148
FINALIST 2
£45.00
6 407 120292 101932A
TO BE RETAINED

WEMBLEY STADIUM
SATURDAY 14TH MAY 1994
FA CUP 1994
ONE HUNDRED AND THIRTEENTH
©THE FOOTBALL ASSOCIATION
TURNSTILE M
BLOCK ROW SEAT
FOOTBALL ASSOCIATION
224 13 56
£60.00
32100 415 190494 163532A
Kick-Off 3.00pm - Turnstiles 1.00pm
Please take your positions by 2.15pm
Special items and conditions of issue apply to this ticket. See the reverse.
TO BE RETAINED

1994

"Football, bloody hell"

"*Fergie's fledglings*" come up trumps for the manager and United gain a historic Treble.

In a year that should have consolidated the growing successes, when Andy Cole and David May arrived at Old Trafford, when Paul Scholes and Gary Neville were able to make their mark on the United side, when Ferguson had become a CBE in the New Year's Honours List, the manager found he needed every ounce of his man-management qualities in dealing with Eric Cantona.

United were fighting for the top spot in January 1995 having been in second position over the previous eight matches, when Cantona's fiery temper exploded during the match with Crystal Palace, and the frenchman Kung Fu kicked an abusive spectator.

Ferguson didn't see the incident that landed his star a £20,000 club fine, a £10,000 FA fine, an eight-month ban and 120 hours of community service. Cantona left for Paris, ready to turn his back on English football.

Ferguson was desperate to keep him at Manchester, and the star himself knew that in England he was reaching his full potential; something that would probably not happen anywhere else. The manager considered this situation to be a state of emergency, and flew to Paris; each man needed the other badly. Cantona had made Ferguson's dream come true; Ferguson had made his striker into a top star and would fight the world, if need be, to get Cantona back.

Cantona relented and returned to the fold.

His ban, however, probably robbed United of the league title, which they conceded to Leeds United by one point. There was no silverware to be had elsewhere, either, as they lost the FA Cup final to Everton 1-0.

Heavy controversy followed in the summer of 1995. Ferguson stuck to his guns and to his philosophy of immediately shedding players that he no longer thought could offer United useful service, for whatever reason.

In later years, he explained a little more about his thinking on this aspect of his management style: *"The goal was to evolve gradually, moving older players out and younger players in... who did we have coming through and where did we see them in three years' time... were there signs that existing players were getting older?"* .

The sweeping out this year included Paul Ince, Mark Hughes and Andrei Kanchelskis. There was puzzlement and anger at the sales without replacements. But the manager had his eye on, and faith in, the new youngsters, *"Fergie's fledglings" as they would be known. Towards the end of his career, Ferguson would credit the revamped youth system for*

-1999

RIGHT: 1996 FA Cup Final, Manchester United 1 v Liverpool 0, Liverpool's Steve McManaman is challenged for the ball by Roy Keane, 11th May 1996

ABOVE: 1996 FA Cup Final, Liverpool's Robbie Fowler in an angry exchange with Manchester United's Roy Keane, 11th May 1996

FA Charity Shield Wembley, Manchester United 4 v Newcastle United 0, David Beckham clashes with John Beresford, 11th August 1996

1996 FA Cup Final, Wembley, Manchester United 1 v Liverpool 0, Alex Ferguson congratulates his captain Eric Cantona after the match, 11th May 1996

" You know, that's life – up and down "

underpinning his success story. He became a father figure to the youngsters and through his encouragement and rock-solid belief in their talents instilled in them an absolute confidence in their own abilities. Fledglings David Beckham, Phil and Gary Neville, Nicky Butt and Paul Scholes were placed in the firing line. History shows how right Ferguson was to put them there despite renewed vitriol from the press. These lads were soon joined by Les Ferdinand and David Ginola to run alongside the restored "King", Cantona, who played again in October.

It wasn't long before this crack squad of 1995/96 had critics eating humble pie (after critics had squawked when the team went down 3-1 to Aston Villa in the first match) and delighted everyone with two runs of ten and then eleven games without defeat as the season rolled on. The losses against the big boys of Liverpool and Arsenal were more than compensated for by the double victories against league runners up Newcastle; 2-0 at home, 1-0 away, with Cantona firing on all cylinders, repaying his boss by scoring the only and winning goals in six matches and the goals that secured a draw in three others. He also earned himself a hug on the field from a delighted Fergie in the process. He didn't score in the 6-0 dismantling of Bolton in February, but he was on the scoresheet again in a blistering 5-0 thrashing of Nottingham Forest in the penultimate match of the season. The side eventually took the title four points clear of Newcastle on 78, with 82 points.

After consuming humble pie, the critics had to eat their words, too, because six days later, *"Fergie's fledglings" were in the FA Cup final against deadly rivals Liverpool. And the man who cracked in the winning goal? King Eric, of course, giving gifts to his adoring subjects. He had been named captain for the game and won the Footballer of the Year award as United became the first team to win the Double twice. The French footballing philosopher's take on it all? "You know, that's life – up and down".*

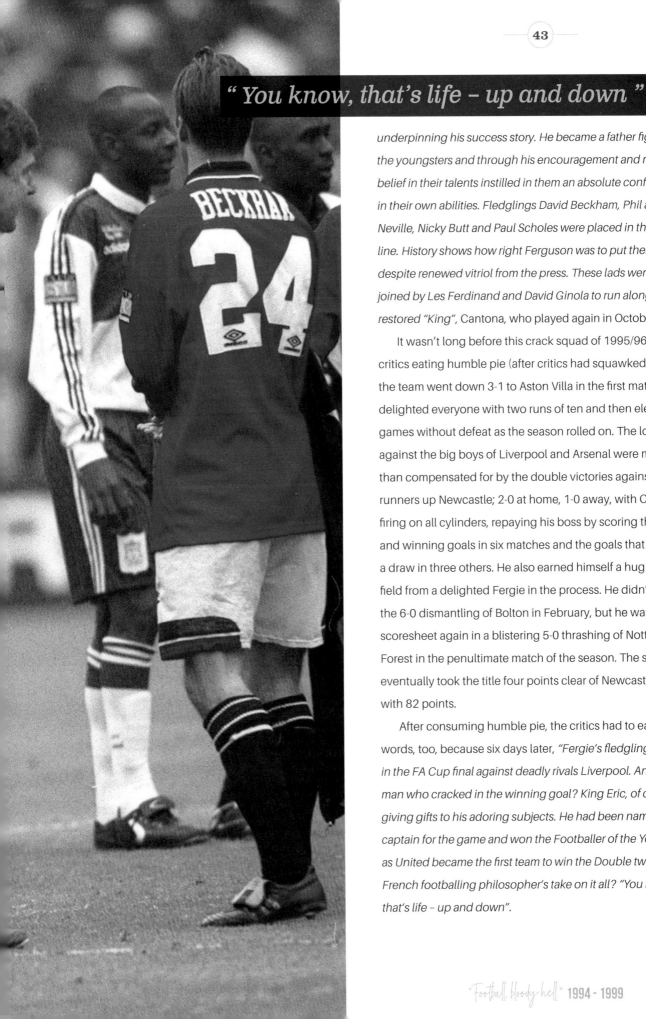

" The Baby-faced Assassin "

As for Ferguson, he signed a four year contract.

Unbeknown to anyone, the Eric and Fergie winning act had just one more show to put on; the 1996/97 season. Ferguson, never a man to rest on his laurels, added more strength to the side with Norwegian forward Ole Gunnar Solskjaer, who acquired the nickname *"The Baby-faced Assassin"*. Beckham was PFA Player of the Year.

Yet, while the season brought in another League title, there was disappointment in the FA Cup, a 1-0 loss to Wimbledon in the fourth round replay, and Europe, where they lost to Borussia Dortmund in the semi-final, 1-0 in each leg of the European Cup.

United lost just five league matches, three of those back-to-back; the worst defeats were two inexplicable collapses against Newcastle, 5-0, in October, and then one week later against Southampton, where they folded 3-6. Whatever Ferguson said to them, it prompted a sixteen-game run without defeat that brought them from sixth to first in the table and they never relinquished the spot again, taking the title with 75 points from Newcastle, Arsenal and Liverpool all on 68.

The sad news was that Eric Cantona had decided that he no longer loved the game enough to continue playing. Four League titles in five years was quite a haul. But the loss of the UEFA Champion's League games to Borussia Dortmund had upset the Frenchman, and within twenty-four hours of that loss, Fergie was told that this time, the great double act was truly over. Bringing eighty-two goals in one hundred and eighty-five appearances, the star had been treated by Ferguson as the football genius that he was and both had profited immensely. Cantona's special relationship

Ole Gunnar Solskjaer is tackled by Thomas Zingler of Rapid Vienna during a Champions League match in Vienna, 4th December 1996

" .. one of the all time greats of world football "

with the boss, who would even break his own rules for the Frenchman, had been accepted by all; there was, in any case, no choice.

But now, that unique era had come to an end, and there was a hole in the side. Ferguson had to decide how to fill it, and fast.

He concluded that new striker Teddy Sheringham from Tottenham Hotspur was the man to follow in Cantona's footsteps for the 1997/98 season. Roy Keane took over as captain.

Irishman Roy Keane had come to Manchester in 1993 with Brian Clough's praises ringing in his ears. Fergie loved Keane's all or nothing attitude that made him a feared opponent, top class in every department, including heading and passing. United had been his dream ever since his youth in Cork. Sought after by other top teams, there was only one team he wanted to join and his talent made him an absolute favourite of the fans for the twelve years he spent there.

Frustrating is probably a euphemistic way to describe Ferguson's new season. United were on the number one spot most of the time, holding their own against Liverpool and Leeds. Meanwhile, in the FA Cup challenge, Manchester had been drawn against Chelsea, who could never be written off with players like Di Mateo and Zola in the team. And it would be a home game for Chelsea.

United began in sparkling form with Giggs causing constant problems in the Blues' defence. Twenty-three minutes in, United were on the move forward again and when Sheringham back headed the ball to Beckham, Beckham darted through to stab the ball into the back of the net for the first goal.

It was a signal for a golden shower of goals. Just six minutes later, Beckham was on target again when his free kick was taken in his classic style, the ball curling around the defensive wall for United's second. Chelsea had little to offer in return and on forty-five minutes, Cole was left unmarked on the halfway line. He took a pass from Giggs and finished his terrific run through the Chelsea half with a sharp and cheeky chip over the Chelsea keeper. 3-0. Chelsea played better when they returned for the second half, but they still couldn't dent the United defence and on the sixty-sixth minute, Cole was attacking the goal again put through by a beautiful Giggs pass that split the defence. In went Cole's seventeenth goal in sixteen games and United's fourth of the afternoon.

And still it wasn't over.

In the seventy-fourth minute, Sheringham was the beneficiary of a lax Chelsea defence and his header from a well-placed floating cross gave United a five-goal lead. At which point United decided it was over. And paid for it. A beautiful lob over Schmeichel's head by Le Saux for a Chelsea consolation goal. So it seemed.

Now it was United's turn to show lax defending, and Vialli was given a wide-open opportunity for Chelsea's second. He took it. Not a problem. Until Pallister caused a disaster with an appalling back pass that was snapped up by Chelsea. With Schmeichel way off his goal line, Vialli made the scoreline 5-3. It was a lesson in how to become dangerously complacent, but fortunately for United they got away with it.

"It's a long season and we will get better in terms of consistency. You have to do that if you want to win the Premiership", said a buoyant United manager.

Even Fergie couldn't get every prediction right. One month later, United crashed out of the FA Cup to Barnsley in the fifth round, 3-4 on aggregate. Little consolation that they beat Barnsley 2-0 in the last league match of the season or that they had destroyed them 7-0 the previous October.

Two fatal losses at home then cost United the

Eric Cantona before the Champions League match against Rapid Vienna in Vienna, 4th Dec 1996

" the best display of finishing in my time at United... "

championship. In that same month of January 1998 when they had beaten Chelsea, it was Leicester City who did the damage, 0-1. In March, the fans had to suffer through a match that gave victory to Arsenal for the second time that season, 0-1. It was heartbreaking, but it gave the London side the championship by one point, 78 to 77.

Having suffered agonising ligament damage early in the season, captain Roy Keane had been absent for the remainder of the season, and Paul Scholes, considered by Cantona to be *"... one of the all time greats of world football"* and a man that Ferguson wanted to help Keane dominate the centre of the field, was now brought up to fill that gap. Scholes was dubbed the *"Ginger Prince"* and with one of the finest brains in football, according to Ferguson, was the frontrunner in the manager's coterie of sharp new talent.

Once again, the critics were quick to put the boot in, seeing United on the slippery slope downwards. Ferguson had no time for such talk. The team had taken on his never-say-die attitude, so he wasn't about to allow the naysayers any breathing space and predicted, rightly, that United would be back and better than ever before. Not even he, perhaps, could have predicted the extraordinary season that was about to unfold at Manchester in the new season. The club and manager would be transformed.

The Dutch player Jaap Stam was considered to be the world's best defender; indeed a one-man defence by fans in Holland. In Manchester, he carved out a name for himself as one of United's most superb defenders, the undisputed star of the defence. Fans would come to adore his huge shape at centre half, where he terrorised the opposition with the authority and pose of a world-class player. His services had been acquired by Fergie in the summer, and he was joined by striker Dwight Yorke, who was to prove his worth over and over, delivering twenty-nine goals in his first season.

Ferguson wanted the lads to lay down the rules from the word go in August 1998 at the Charity Shield match against Arsenal. Roy Keane was back in the side, too. United sank without trace, 3-0. Neither was the start in the League much better with two draws against Leicester City and West Ham United upsetting fans to the extent that stones and bottles were thrown and David Beckham was booed when he touched the ball. United slipped to eleventh place. Despondency spread, except in Fergie's head. Wait till the new boys had settled in, he cautioned.

And suddenly the team threw off the invisible cloak.

From that point on they lost just three games; to Arsenal 3-0, Sheffield Wednesday 3-1, and Middlesbrough 3-2. They hammered in four in each of the games against Charlton, Everton and West Ham, five against Wimbledon, six against Leicester and eight against Nottingham Forest. That game was the first for the new assistant Steve McLaren, Ferguson's own first choice. Within seven minutes, three goals had been scored, first by Yorke for United, then Rogers for Forest then Cole for United. But after that whirlwind opening, it was United who settled and began to dominate the game, held off, it must be said, by a determined Forest defence.

But after the break, the avalanche began and Forest were buried. Ferguson, naturally delighted, praised his team and especially Ole Gunnar Solskjaer, who had whacked in four goals within ten minutes of each other. *"It was", he declared, "the best display of finishing in my time at United... we have never been stronger".*

He was right about that but United still had a fight on their hands as they aimed for glory, because Arsenal and Chelsea refused to be bowed by the United strikers, and the League battle continued right up until May 1999 and the third last game of the season when they hit the top spot.

Ryan Giggs celebrates after scoring the winning goal during the FA Cup Semi Final match between Manchester United and Arsenal at Villa Park , 4th April 1999

" We deserved our success, we are the best team in the country "

Giggs had scored what must be one of the most gorgeous goals ever, during the Arsenal match, when he took a loose ball from his own half, thrust forward past two Arsenal men into the Arsenal half, held off two challenges from Keown and Adams and released a rocket-propelled shot into the roof of Seaman's net after a run of sixty yards.

"Genius", said Ferguson. "It's his balance that gives him the chance of being truly great", adding that his goal would go down as one of the greatest of all time. Giggs himself thought it his best-ever goal.

A 0-0 result against Blackburn Rovers almost crippled them at the second last hurdle but they hung on to beat Tottenham Hotspur in the final game and pip Arsenal to the post by a single point, 79 to 78. The fifth title in seven years.

"We deserved our success, we are the best team in the country", purred Fergie, but warned, *"The club is not about egos... I will make sure no one gets carried away"*.

One week later and the FA Cup final beckoned them after a gruelling campaign in which they had again been pitted against Arsenal and Chelsea and won only after a replay each time. Newcastle United were the opponents in the final.

United took the lead and didn't seem likely to lose it for most of the game. They added a second in the second half and lifted the FA Cup for the Double, the third in five years. This elicited an understated *"The boys were marvellous... a tremendous season"*, from Ferguson.

Now there was another prize to concentrate on; United had battled Europe's best teams, including Internazionale and Juventus to reach the final of the UEFA Champion's League competition.

Their opposition in the final was the feared German side

Barcelona, Champions League 98/99 Final, against Bayern Munich. Ryan Giggs takes on Michael Tarnat & Oliver Kahn, 26th May 1999

" The club is not about egos... "

Bayern Munich. Ferguson was confident that he had as good a team as any English side that had ever been in the final.

"I will be the happiest man in the world if we win", he commented.

After six minutes of play, he was probably the most miserable as Bayern scored with a curling free kick. There was no Keane, no Scholes; Beckham and Giggs were meant to plug the gaps, but the midfield was Bayern territory and United did not look as though it was going to be their day. Bayern felt safe to rely on their midfield.

The second half rolled on and the minutes ticked. On sixty-six minutes, Ferguson pushed Giggs and Beckham out to the flanks. To no avail, the Germans were still dangerous. Ten minutes left and Solskjaer came on. On eighty-nine minutes, United hearts were on the floor and the Germans were already celebrating. But the lads still wouldn't give up.

Then it happened.

A United corner.

Beckham to Yorke to Giggs and then it was Sheringham who had the ball in the net. Uproar in the stands, Bayern grim, United going all out for goal to make the unbelievable become reality. The United wave surged forward and won another corner. Beckham to Sheringham, and that golden moment when Solskjaer's foot pushed the ball into the roof of the net. And then the game was over. An incredible finish to an incredible season.

Astonished, as was everyone else, Ferguson could do no

The Manchester United team line up with the European Cup trophy after their dramatic win, 26th May 1999

more than exclaim, *"Football, bloody football... unbelievable. I'm so proud of my players"*. His players, he enthused, were *"... incredible human beings... when you've got that spirit, it's incredible"*. It was the best night of his and his team's lives; United had won the Treble, just the fourth team in history to do so, unbeaten in all European matches and losing just four domestic games.

Many, many years later, Ferguson said in an interview, *"People continually say to me, 'What was your finest moment?' and it's always Barcelona (The Champions League final, 1999)... that to me, was the crowning moment in terms of I'd never won the Champions League before... that was a great moment, and the way we did it will never be forgotten, 1-0 down with three minutes left in injury time and we win it. So it was an amazing moment, and it reflected also the character of Manchester United, they never gave in. That was the greatest example in the final"*.

For Peter Schmeichel, the rock in the goalmouth, it was his last United game, an incredible send off for a superb goalkeeper. Fans would certainly miss his huge frame that seemed to block the space between the posts, or the long, pin-point-accurate throw outs by a keeper acknowledged as one of the world's elite players, which started many attacks.

For Ferguson, the most successful football manager ever, the Queen had a knighthood ready.

Sir Alex modestly said that, of course, there were many people who had made the club the greatest in the world. Of course. But he was the magic glue that held them all together to produce those wonderful victories.

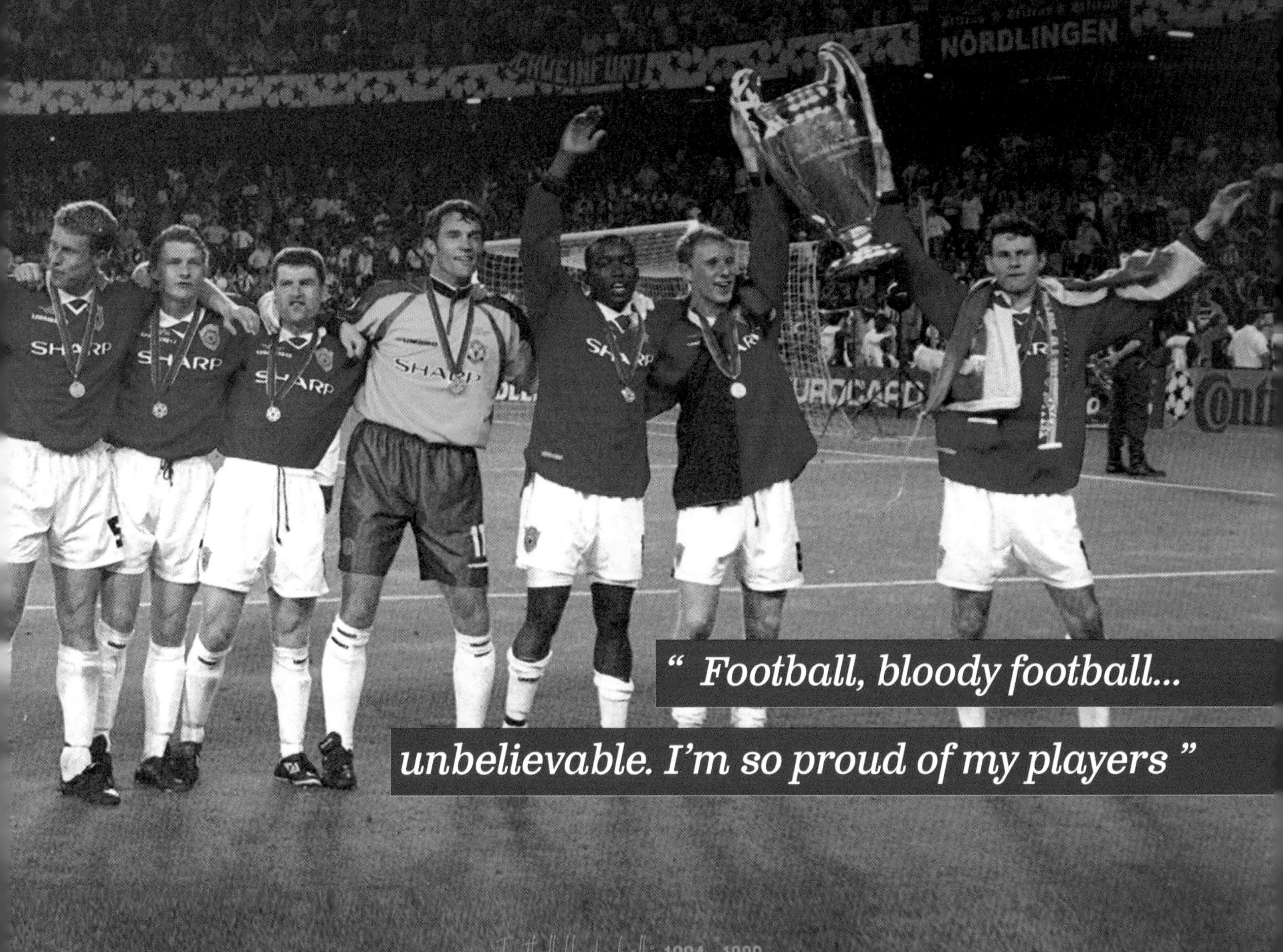

" Football, bloody football... unbelievable. I'm so proud of my players "

THE 1995 F.A. CUP FINAL
SPONSORED BY LITTLEWOODS POOLS
LITTLEWOODS
LITTLEWOODS
Everton V Manchester United
WEMBLEY
STADIUM LIMITED
SATURDAY 20 MAY KICK-OFF 3.00PM
Official Matchday Programme £5.00

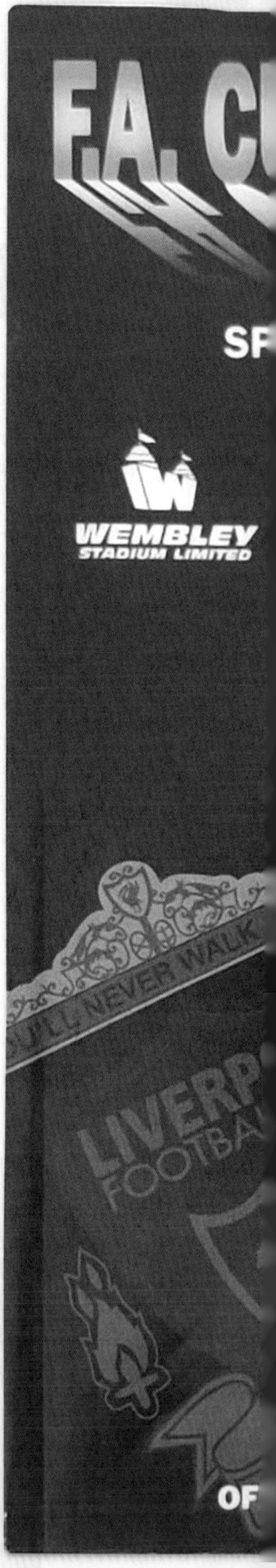
WEMBLEY
STADIUM LIMITED

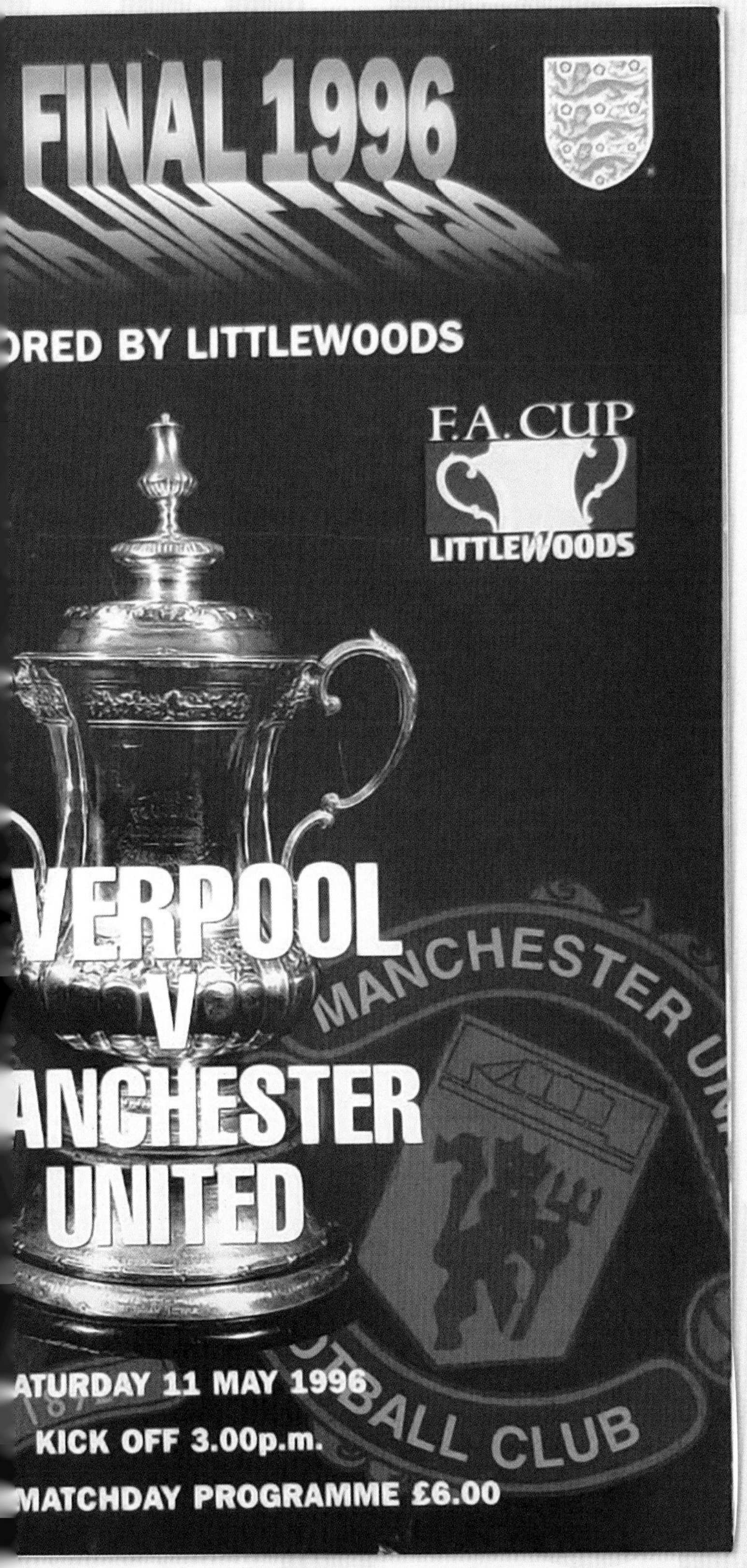
FINAL 1996
ORED BY LITTLEWOODS
F.A. CUP
LITTLEWOODS
VERPOOL
V
ANCHESTER
UNITED
MANCHESTER UN
ALL CLUB
ATURDAY 11 MAY 1996
KICK OFF 3.00p.m.
MATCHDAY PROGRAMME £6.00

WEMBLEY STADIUM
SATURDAY 20TH MAY 1995
LITTLEWOODS POOLS
THE FOOTBALL ASSOCIATION CHALLENGE CUP
Sponsored by Littlewoods Pools FINAL TIE 1995
PLEASE TAKE YOUR POSITIONS BY 2.15PM. TURNSTILES OPEN AT 1.00PM. KICK-OFF AT 3.00PM
TURNSTILE J
BLOCK ROW SEAT
140 10 171
£17.00
FINALIST 2
TO BE RETAINED

WEMBLEY STADIUM
SATURDAY 11TH MAY 1996
The Football Association
Challenge Cup
THE FINAL TIE
1996
Sponsored by
F.A. CUP SPONSOR
LITTLEWOODS
KICK OFF 3.00PM - TURNSTILES 1.00PM
PLEASE TAKE YOUR SEATS BY 2.15PM
BLOCK ROW SEAT
125 16 26
TURNSTILE M
HAMPSHIRE F.A.
£30.00
TO BE RETAINED

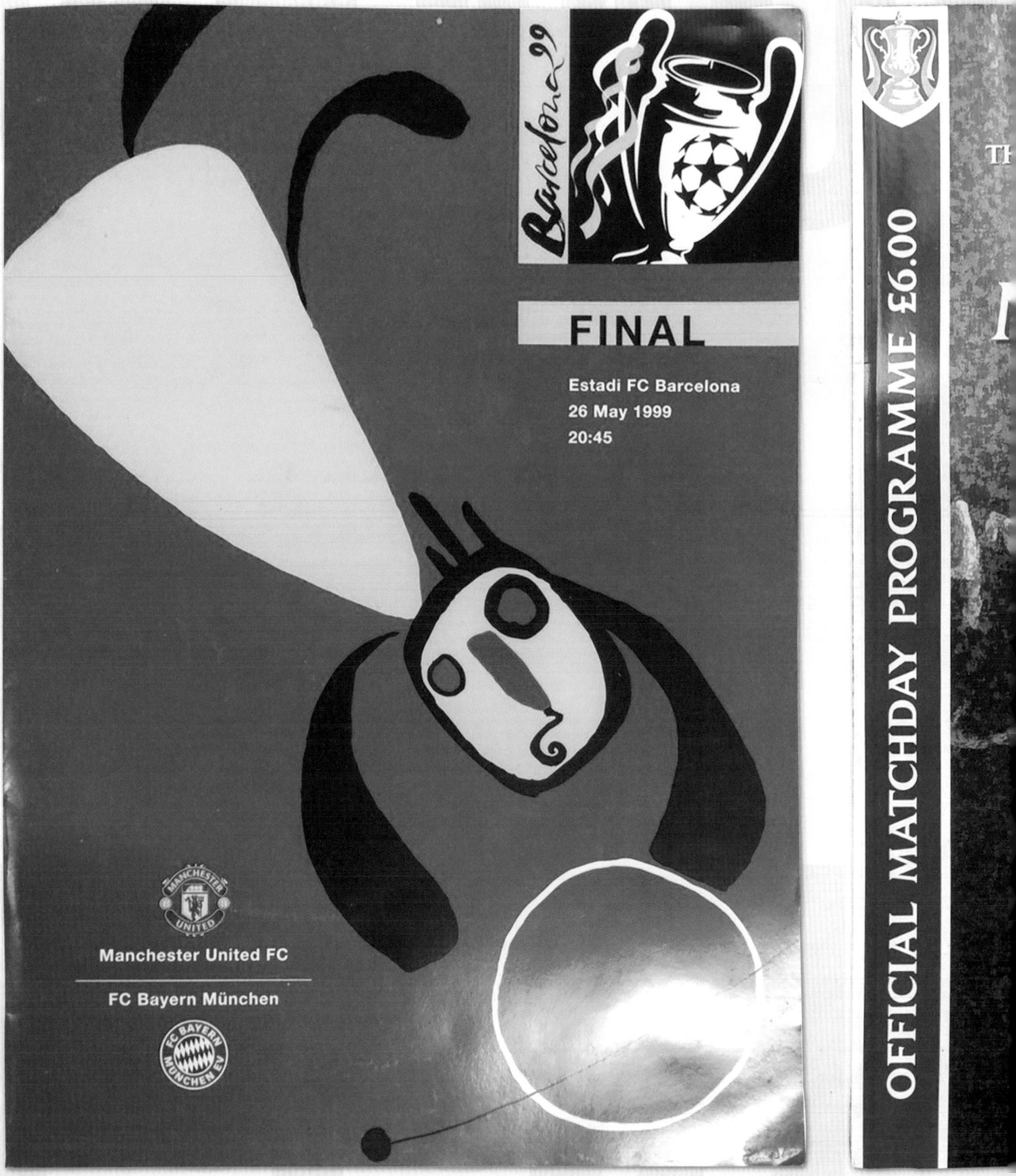
Barcelona 99
FINAL
Estadi FC Barcelona
26 May 1999
20:45
Manchester United FC
FC Bayern München
OFFICIAL MATCHDAY PROGRAMME £6.00

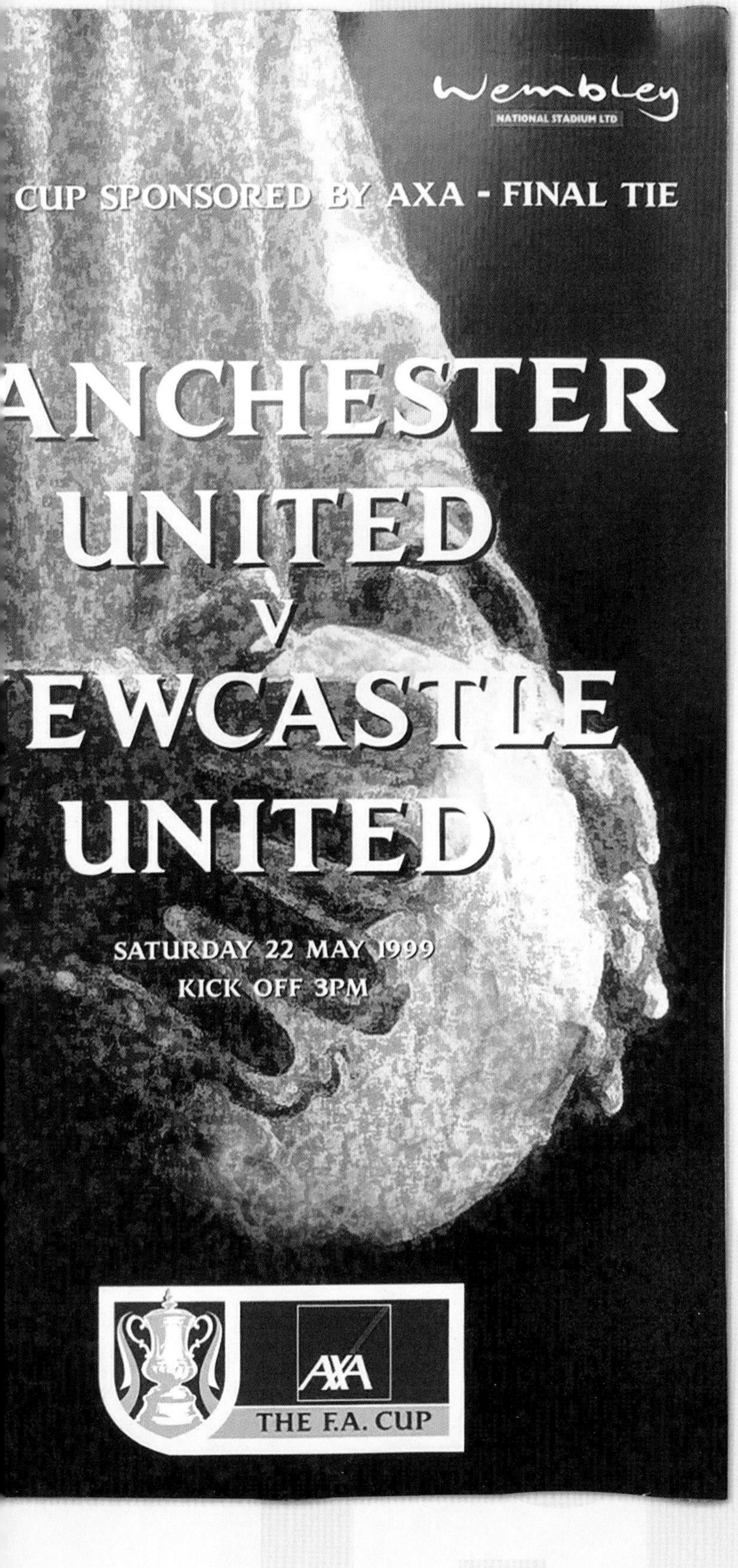
Wembley
NATIONAL STADIUM LTD
CUP SPONSORED BY AXA - FINAL TIE
ANCHESTER
UNITED
v
EWCASTLE
UNITED
SATURDAY 22 MAY 1999
KICK OFF 3PM
AXA
THE F.A. CUP

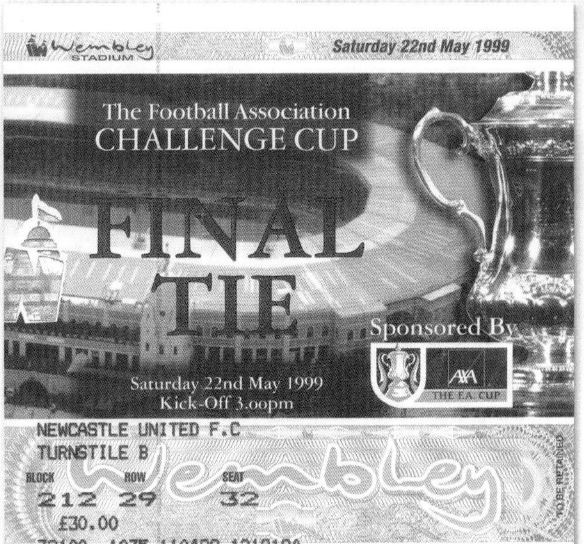
Wembley STADIUM
Saturday 22nd May 1999
The Football Association
CHALLENGE CUP
FINAL
TIE
Sponsored By
AXA
THE F.A. CUP
Saturday 22nd May 1999
Kick-Off 3.00pm
NEWCASTLE UNITED F.C
TURNSTILE B
BLOCK ROW SEAT
212 29 32
£30.00
32100 1035 110499 121918A

77
J267A0
FINAL UEFA CHAMPIONS LEAGUE'99
ESTADI FC BARCELONA, 26 MAY 1999, 20:45
GOL NORD 2 GRADERIA
MANCHESTER UNITED FC
v
FC BAYERN MUNCHEN
MANCHESTER UNITED FC
021147
CHAMPIONS LEAGUE
PUERTA/PORTA: 9 BOCA/BOCA:345 FILA/FILA: 0029 ASIENTO/SEIENT: 0001 PRECIO/PREU: 7000 PTS

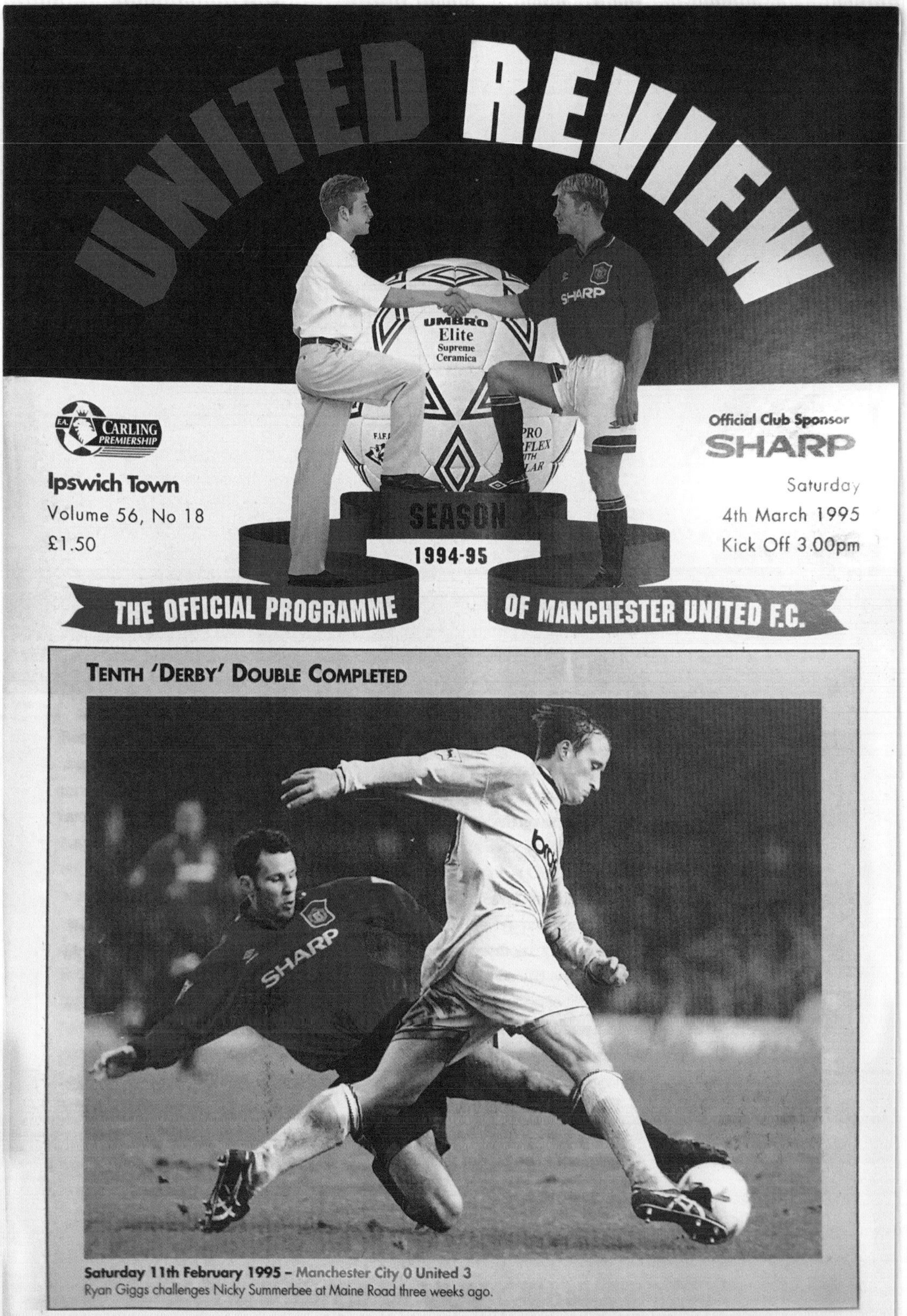
UNITED REVIEW
UMBRO
Elite
Supreme
Ceramica
SHARP
CARLING PREMIERSHIP
Ipswich Town
Volume 56, No 18
£1.50
SEASON
1994-95
Official Club Sponsor
SHARP
Saturday
4th March 1995
Kick Off 3.00pm
THE OFFICIAL PROGRAMME
OF MANCHESTER UNITED F.C.
TENTH 'DERBY' DOUBLE COMPLETED
SHARP
Saturday 11th February 1995 – Manchester City 0 United 3
Ryan Giggs challenges Nicky Summerbee at Maine Road three weeks ago.

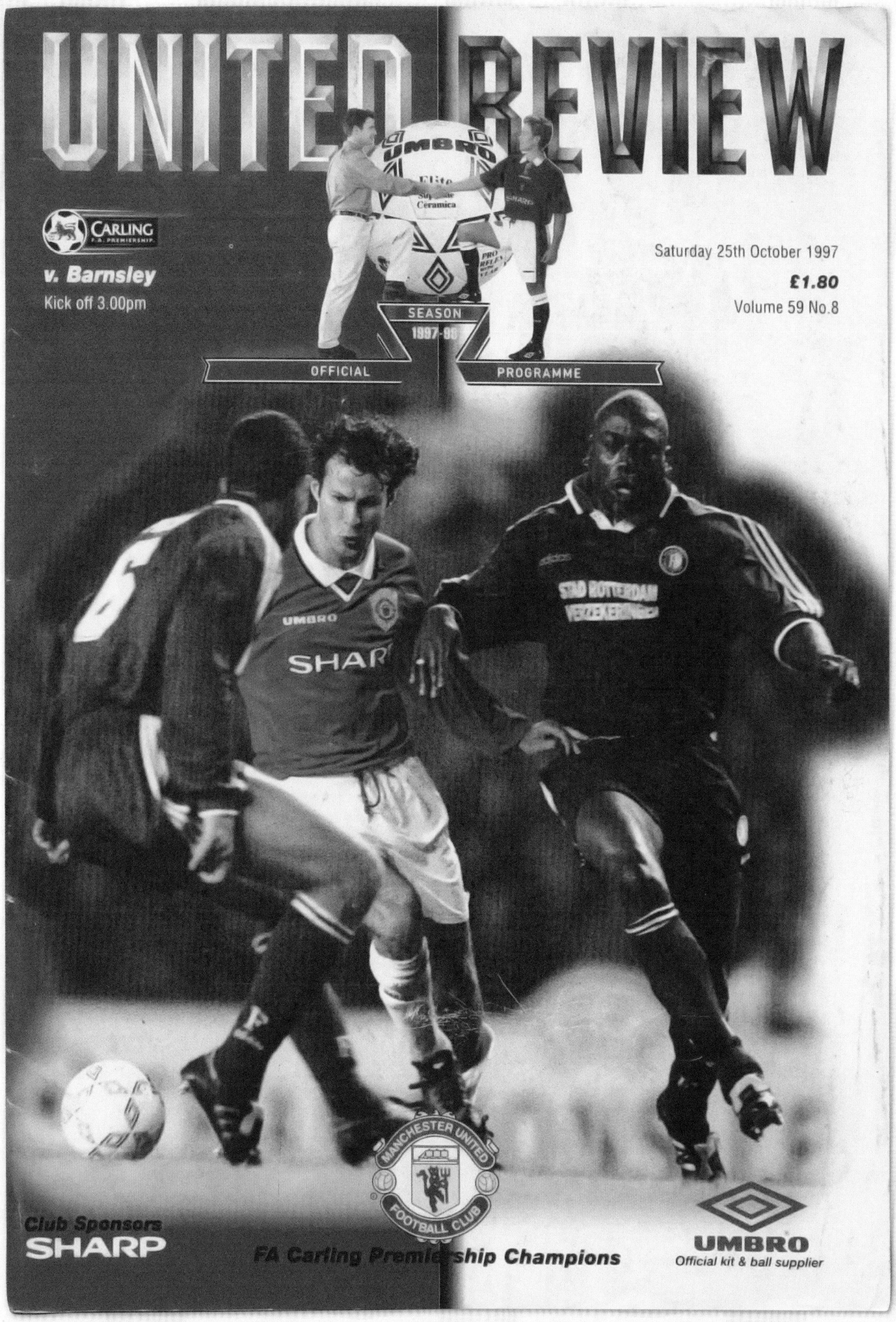
UNITED REVIEW
CARLING F.A. PREMIERSHIP
v. Barnsley
Kick off 3.00pm
Saturday 25th October 1997
£1.80
Volume 59 No.8
SEASON
1997-98
OFFICIAL
PROGRAMME
UMBRO
SHARP
MANCHESTER UNITED FOOTBALL CLUB
Club Sponsors
SHARP
FA Carling Premiership Champions
UMBRO
Official kit & ball supplier

1999: I will retire – but not yet

Ferguson decides to retire but then changes his mind. He describes his biggest mistake at the club as "*... letting go of Jaap Stam*".

Alex Ferguson knew that he could not escape the close presence of the past that he had been entrusted to nurture. Not that he wanted to or felt threatened by it. For him, managing Manchester United was *"... about building on the bedrock laid down by Sir Matt Busby"*. He also knew that the ball never stops rolling in football; yesterday's success means nothing in tomorrow's match. Ferguson's unique skill was to constantly regenerate a successful team, keep it's life blood flowing by jettisoning those in the club who were no longer able or willing to pull their weight; to rebuild cup-winning sides. This required constant homework because Ferguson asked himself how a player would be performing three years down the line, and acted accordingly. Now, after such glorious success, would the players be suffering from an inflated sense of self-worth or would they be able to put the astonishing year behind them, start from scratch as he did?

As it turned out the season was sweet and sour. Let's get the sour out the way first...

There would be no FA Cup competition in the 1999/2000 season because the club had decided to play in the FIFA World Club Championship instead, much to the chagrin of many people. After a promising start, the defence of the European title crashed landed against Real Madrid, 0-0 and 3-2 in the quarter-final. Having deprived fans of their team in the FA Cup run, United didn't progress past the group stage in the FIFA Club World Championship.

The team was essentially the same as the Treble-winning side minus Peter Schmeichel, who was replaced by Mark Bosnich, and then, when he proved a disappointment, Italian Massimo Taibi. Taibi could not fill the great Schmeichel's shoes, either. Fortunately, the men in front of the goal were still eager to bring in the trophies.

On the sweet side, United set out to defend the Premiership title and fortunately the figures speak for themselves. They lost just three games in the league, one when they were drubbed embarrassingly by Chelsea 5-0 in October 1999 (with Massimo Taibi in goal) having beaten

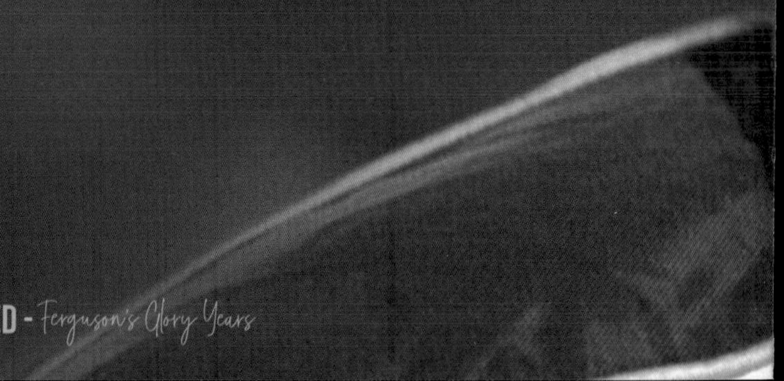

2004

Newcastle 5-1 just a few weeks before. They more than compensated with some terrific results later: 5-1 against Everton; 4-0 against Bradford City, twice; 7-1 against West Ham; 4-0 against Sunderland; eight games where they hit three goals and fourteen games atop the table and without defeat to the end of the season. United claimed their sixth Premiership title ahead of Arsenal by a record eighteen points, with 91.

Unsurprisingly, Taibi did not survive the season and Bosnich was gone by January 2001. By then, French keeper Fabien Alain Barthez had been brought in and the weak link in the goalmouth was finally repaired. The showman keeper was an immediate hit and not only delighted the crowds with his off-the-line antics but saved the team's bacon on more than one occasion with the immediacy of his reactions.

Altogether, an odd season loomed up for United. For Ferguson the year would bring a record-breaking fourteenth major trophy, which put him on the throne of immortals, above Liverpool's Bob Paisley, when United took the Premiership title for the seventh time. No other manager in English football had achieved this, and he was now the most successful manager of all time in English football.

Once again, the side had sailed above Arsenal, beating them to the title by ten points, 80 to 70. They had been on top for all but four games and were sufficiently secure by May to lose the final three. But the FA and League Cups went elsewhere and Bayern Munich took revenge in the UEFA Champion's League by eliminating United in the quarter-finals, 1-0 and 1-2. Ferguson was particularly distressed by this defeat having considered that the team was good enough to take the trophy again.

No one quite realised just how badly the boss took that defeat until on the 18th May 2001, he declared that he was going to *"sever all ties"* with the club and retire after the end of the next season.

The football world went into shock.

One reason Ferguson cited was age, the *"psychological barrier"* of 60, and friction between him and the club did the rest. The fans protested. The group of shareholders known as Shareholders United spoke for many when they pointed out that Ferguson was a strong believer in football being a game run in the interests of the supporters and local communities and not sold out to merchandising and marketing. Manchester United PLC was at odds with this view they maintained and should be ashamed of themselves for what had happened.

The impassioned debate suddenly had the wind taken out of its sails when early in the new year of 2002, Ferguson changed his mind.

Cathy his wife, he commented, *"... could sense I'd made a mistake, she knew I'd made a mistake, and I knew myself. The silly thing was it was impulse, in the heat of the moment. I just decided and I made it at the beginning of the season, which was even worse"*.

She had, apparently, *"kicked"* him when he was sleeping on the couch at home. He awoke to find his wife and sons with their families staring at him and heard his wife say, *"You're not retiring, you're too young to retire"*.

Later, the Scot admitted that it was one of the biggest mistakes he had made at the club as it made the period between then and 2005 when the three-year contract he signed in 2002 expired, much more difficult. The decision to make a public announcement was an *"absolute disaster"* he confessed.

So, no retirement; but he was going to reduce the pressure and workload, change his working day lifestyle somewhat. Writer Frank Worrall also mentions that Ferguson had nightmares about the way Bill Shankly had been treated after retirement, made to feel unwelcome at training sessions,

“ The silly thing was it was impulse. In the heat of the moment … ”

Fabien Barthez of Manchester United during a Premiership match against Bradford City played at Valley Parade, 13th Jan 2001

and also that Sven-Göran Eriksson would take over.

Nonetheless, he repeated the *"mistake"* again immediately by announcing that when the three-year contract was up *"that will be it... I have no intention of staying on at the club in any capacity whatsoever"*.

Oh, Sir Alex. Even managers need managers sometimes it seems.

He was right about the disruption he was causing, though, as the club sought a new manager and a new assistant trainer when Steve McClaren left. There were rumours of problems between Dwight Yorke and the manager, ostensibly because of Yorke's relationship with Jordan, the British model and Yorke was only used intermittently that year, finally leaving when the season was over.

Ryan Giggs had now been at United for over ten years as the 2001/2002 season took off... and the season rather left United behind. It was barely underway before Fergie administered another shock to the club's nervous system by announcing the sale of Jaap Stam in August 2001. His replacement was the aging Laurent Blanc. What had got into Fergie? Had the Dutchman expressed discontent? When Stam later wrote an autobiography, the Daily Mirror newspaper quoted him as writing: *"It's got to the stage where he has even told us: "Don't try and stay on your feet if you're in the box and get a slight kick"*. The player went on to state his difficulties with that policy designed to equal the Italian and Spanish *"flyers"* in European matches.

Whatever the cause of the abrupt departure, Ferguson later admitted that without question, he had made one of the biggest mistakes of his career. It was, he said in his autobiography, *"... such a misjudgment on my part to let Jaap go"*. The manager didn't seem to be thinking straight at all and the results could be seen on the field. A weak start turned into a terrible autumn and winter with United winning just one game out of seven and losing five between October and December, which dropped them to ninth in the table. The recovery began on December 12th when United walloped in five against Derby and six against Southampton shortly after. Another winning streak in the new year of 2002 saw them net four goals each match against Bolton, Sunderland and Tottenham and then five against West Ham. They were back on top of the table.

Until Middlesbrough beat them 1-0 at home. They dropped to second. Not even new boy Ruud van Nistelrooy's thirty-six season goals could turn the tide. Even though United won the next four games. Then Arsenal put in the knife at home again, 1-0 in the penultimate game of a season which finished with a droopy 0-0 draw against Charlton Athletic. The club eventually came home third behind Liverpool, with Arsenal as champions on 87, 10 points clear of United, the Red Devils' lowest Premiership position ever.

Every trophy eluded them. It was the loss of the European Cup in the semi-final to German side Bayer Leverkusen that floored both Keane and Ferguson, both of them still desperate for European glory. Tempers flared and accusations by Keane of players interested only in a bling culture surfaced, of *"cover ups"* and players needing to *"... stand up and be counted"*. The indirect criticism of the boss was not conducive to good relationships.

Putting that dismal season behind them, having said goodbye to Andy Cole and with a new defender to bolster them at the back – Rio Ferdinand, a signing from Leeds United of almost £30 million – the Red Devils did not start as they meant to go on in 2002/03, winning just two matches out of the first six.

But they continued to stutter as they had started, anyway.

Jaap Stam challenges Real Madrid's Raul in a UEFA Champions League quarter-final second-leg match at Old Trafford 19th April 2000

> *" Cristiano is one of the most exciting young players I have ever seen "*

It took until the 28th December for the manager's oil to start working and the team began to pile on the pressure, taking out Newcastle United 6-2 and Liverpool 4-0 during an eighteen-game run without defeat to the end of the season. They pushed perennial rivals Arsenal down into second place, having whittled down their eight-point lead, to take another Premiership title; 83 to 78 points. But the fly in the ointment – two of them, in fact, in separate jars – was losing to Real Madrid in the quarter-finals of the UEFA Champions' League and, accompanied by great gnashing of teeth, losing to Liverpool 0-2 in the League Cup final.

Another year of success, then, but not the high standard of success that everyone at Manchester craved and demanded almost as a birthright.

And there was trouble off the pitch, too. Apart from Keane. David Beckham was proving to be another danger zone.

Ever since his arrival in 1993 as a schoolboy, Becks had made his presence felt, rising to be one of the greats at the club. From out on the right wing, his inch-accurate floating lobs were legendary. Becks had learned from Cantona that hard work was required, and although the world derided him as just a handsome attachment to his pop-star wife, he earned his place and reputation in the team and Fergie stood by him. The manager found Beckham to be one of the only players whose mistakes either never bothered him or were never considered to be mistakes by the player. Fergie admired that, although non-acceptance of reality later became a problem when Becks was no longer the player he used to be. There was never a dent in his confidence when play didn't run in his favour, and he was always eager for the ball whatever happened. And something else that endeared him to the manager was making sure that he was the fittest man in the team. Fergie was always on hand to give advice and guidance; until he felt that the player was more interested in the England shirt than the United one, and the celebrity lifestyle began to irk the no-nonsense Scot. Ferguson's protégé had once loved the game, *"football mad"* was the term used. But the boss watched with growing consternation as Beckham showed that he would prefer to give it all up for a new career; stardom.

By 2002, the father-son relationship that had stood them both in such good stead had disintegrated. There were rumours that they now barely spoke to one another. Ferguson regarded him as a *"celebrity footballer"*, a pejorative term in the Scotsman's eyes, obviously. Worse still, Becks' wife Victoria now supplied almost all of the footballers' advisors. Injured in the early part of the season, Becks' contribution was severely curtailed for a while.

Almost as though Ferguson was punishing him, the manager left Beckham out of the UEFA Champions League match against Real Madrid in April 2003. Until the writing was on the wall and Becks was put on to score two goals in the 4-3 victory. It was ironic, then, that as the season died, Beckham departed after eight years as a first-team regular, to

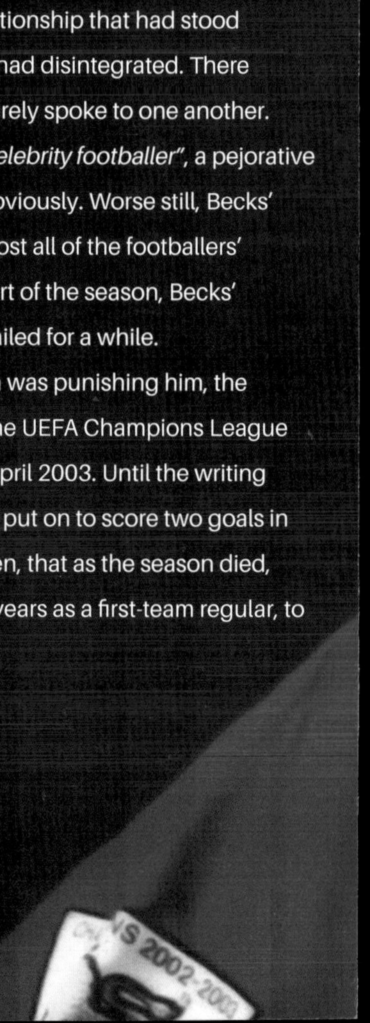

Cristiano Ronaldo during a Premiership match against Chelsea and at Stamford Bridge on 30th November 2003

ABOVE: Cristiano Ronaldo of Manchester United tries a shot during the FA Cup match against Manchester City at Old Trafford, 14th February 2004

RIGHT: Ruud van Nistelrooy celebrates scoring their fourth goal with John O'Shea during FA Cup match against Manchester City at Old Trafford, 14th February 2004

" When you are thinking about the future it is easier to construct that model with younger players "

join none other than Real Madrid.

Beckham was going to be a hard act to follow and his departure ushered in a subsequent dip in United's fortunes.

In a season when Ferguson bought players of the calibre of Portuguese Cristiano Ronaldo and Cameroonian Eric Djemba-Djemba to United, it was to be expected that great things might happen on the field of play. Ferguson was confident. Bolton went down 4-0 in the opening game and hopes rose that this victory could be the herald of good times. Eighteen-year-old Ronaldo had the crowd mesmerised with his ball skills and his boss gave high praise; *"Cristiano is one of the most exciting young players I have ever seen"*. Probably the most exciting anyone had ever seen, in fact, and certainly the most gifted player, Ferguson confessed, that he had managed. But at the time Ferguson was suffering from a bout of wishful thinking, because the youngster was not yet the best player in the world that he was to become; he was still just potential on legs, potent but unfinished, wasting chances in firework displays that got the team nowhere as he tried to show off with his skills. Ferguson's assistant, Carlos Queiroz, worked long and hard with Ronaldo and finally succeeded in making him change from a selfish upstart to one of the world's best players. But at that point, without Beckham, van Nistelrooy was adrift, and a dangerous scenario was arising. Ferguson was sticking to his policy of drafting in youngsters, slotting them in as the stars aged; Roy Keane, who was 32, Ryan Giggs, Ole Gunnar Solskjaer.

"When you are thinking about the future it is easier to construct that model with younger players", opined the boss.

After he had retired, Ferguson spoke more about his philosophy of bringing younger players along in their careers: *"A constant in our discussions about young players was whether they could handle the demands of the Old Trafford crowd... would they grow or shrink in the United shirt?"*. The aspiring young players were scrutinised and graded before they were allowed anywhere near first-team action. *"... we aimed to be sure about their temperaments, sure about their characters and sure of their abilities"*.

Djemba-Djemba failed to fulfill his promise, and defensively the team had a weak spot so that Keane had his work cut out during the Bolton match to keep the opposing forwards out. Only one up at half time, a few choice Scottish phrases to the United team in the dressing room then did the trick.

Still, after winning three games out of four the manager was content. Little did he know that he had entered the dark lands of the doldrums. It had not, of course, escaped Ferguson's notice that the cogs were not working as smoothly together as they should have been; that he was having difficulty in establishing stability in various aspects of the team with Paul Scholes and Ryan Giggs getting older and without a player of Beckham's ability.

The dreams flared only briefly, in December 2003 and early January 2004 when the team was on top of the League for five weeks. That was it. Even though van Nistelrooy eventually fired in thirty goals, the Red Devils, ominously, were unable to crack Arsenal again or Chelsea and any feelings of foreboding turned out to be justified. Eight games passed without a goal for the Manchester side. They were third again behind Chelsea and champions Arsenal after the last match in May 2004.

No European glory this time out, either. Porto saw United off 4-3 on aggregate in the Champions League, and the game cost Keane a red card for stamping on the Portuguese keeper

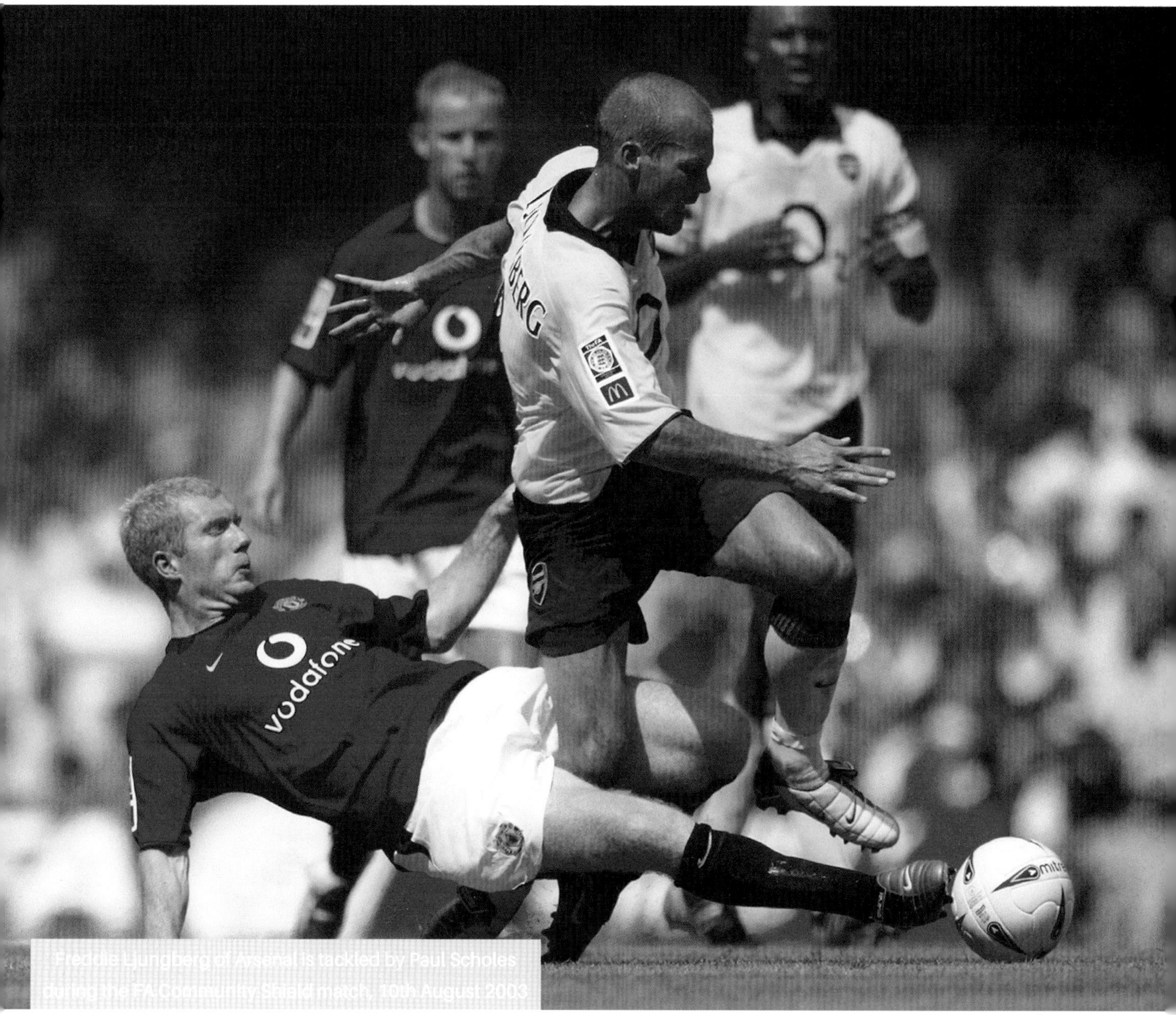

Freddie Ljungberg of Arsenal is tackled by Paul Scholes during the FA Community Shield match, 10th August 2003

three minutes from time. Ferguson defended his player saying, oddly, *"... there was no malice in the incident"*. The Porto manager, none other than José Mourinho, replied, *"I can understand why he is a bit emotional. You would be sad if your team gets as clearly dominated by opponents who have been built on ten percent of the budget"*.

The only ray of light gleamed from the Community Shield when Arsenal had been subdued 4-3 on penalties, and the Cup final – by now, Ronaldo was making his scintillating presence truly felt – when League One side Millwall were sent packing 3-0 after Arsenal had again been humbled 1-0 in the semi-final. A record eleventh win for the club. A successful year for anyone not named Alex Ferguson. *"I am very pleased for the players and the fans"*, he said afterwards not forgetting to praise Ronaldo, whose performance he called *"outstanding"*.

A pity that Arsenal's revenge came in the shape of the Premiership title; fifteen points clear of United. Dissatisfaction emerged amongst the fans.

Manchester United celebrate with the FA Cup after beating Millwall at the Millennium Stadium, 22nd May 2004

" I am very pleased for the players and the fans "

And then, something akin to a blackout descended on United.

What happened? Certainly Rio Ferdinand had a hand in the slide when he got himself banned for failing to attend a drugs test in January 2004. Eight months off the field. He had walked out of the club after the test had been asked for at the training ground. Whatever the suspicions that gave rise to, at the very least the ban helped to scupper Fergie's hopes of European success.

And then Fergie got involved in legal proceedings. As the part owner of a racehorse, Rock of Gibraltar, with the wife of one of the football club's majority shareholders, when his name was missing on the list of owners at the time the colt went to stud, he felt cheated. John Magnier, the shareholder in question, struck back and raised doubts about Ferguson's transfer deals in the club and spoke in derogatory terms about the manager's behaviour generally. It was a dangerous moment for the Scot. The air was eventually cleared, out of court, but the affair had cast a shadow over the club for far too long, raising the prospect of Ferguson being fired. The threat of the loss of an irreplaceable manager unsettled everyone; damage had been done to confidence all round.

Another blight that settled on everyone was the expected takeover of the club by Paul Glazer, who would pile his debts onto United. If the manager stayed, what purchasing power would he have? Would he be ousted by the new management? More unwanted uncertainty swilled around Old Trafford.

The FA
COMMUNITY SHIELD
IN PARTNERSHIP WITH McDONALD'S
ARSENAL v MANCHESTER UNITED
2PM SUNDAY, 10 AUGUST 2003
MILLENNIUM STADIUM, CARDIFF
The FA
COMMUNITY SHIELD
PRESENTING PARTNER
£5 OFFICIAL MATCHDAY PROGRAMME
TheFA.com
NSPCC

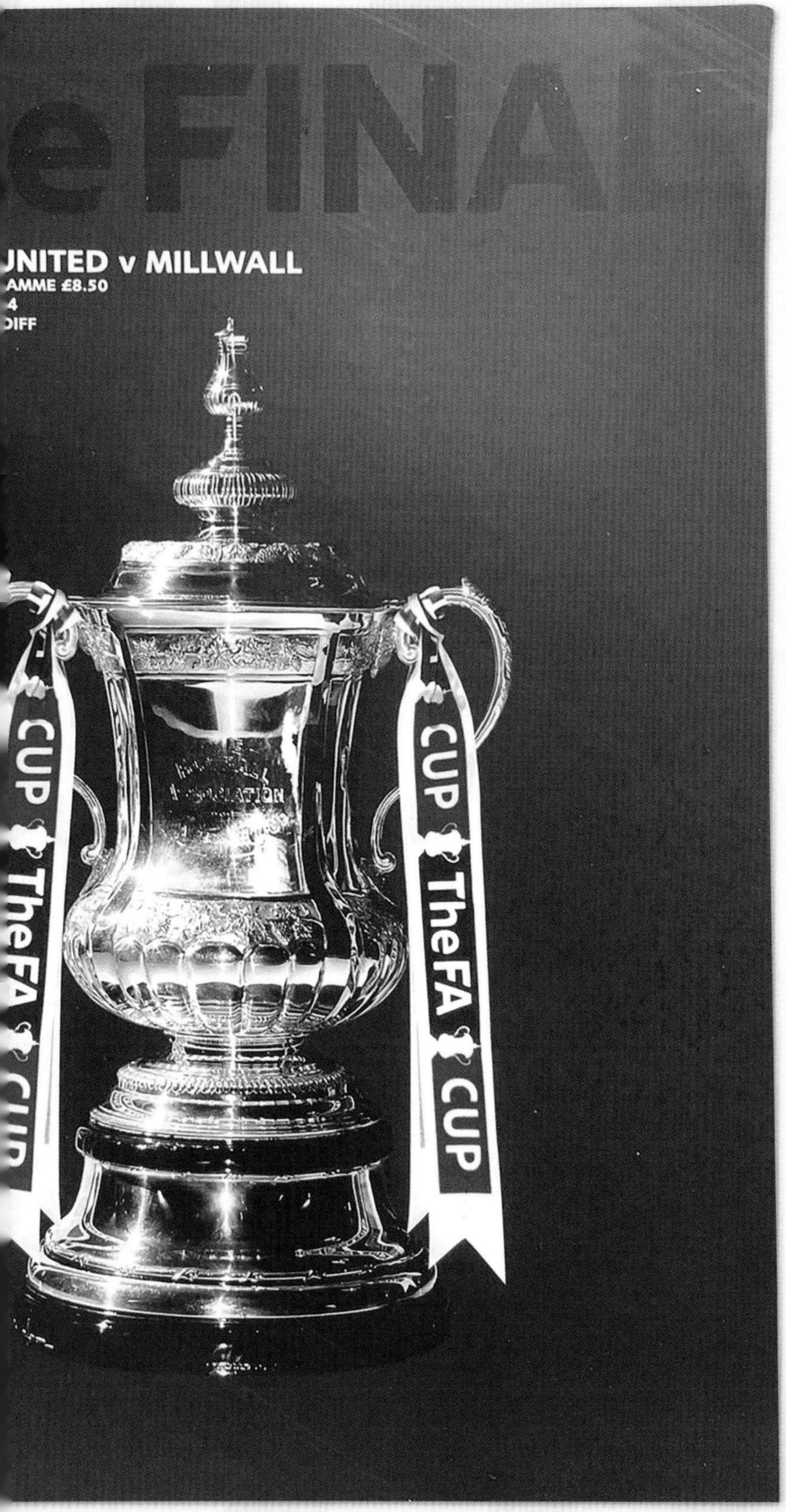
eFINAL
UNITED v MILLWALL
AMME £8.50
4
DIFF
CUP TheFA CUP
CUP TheFA CUP

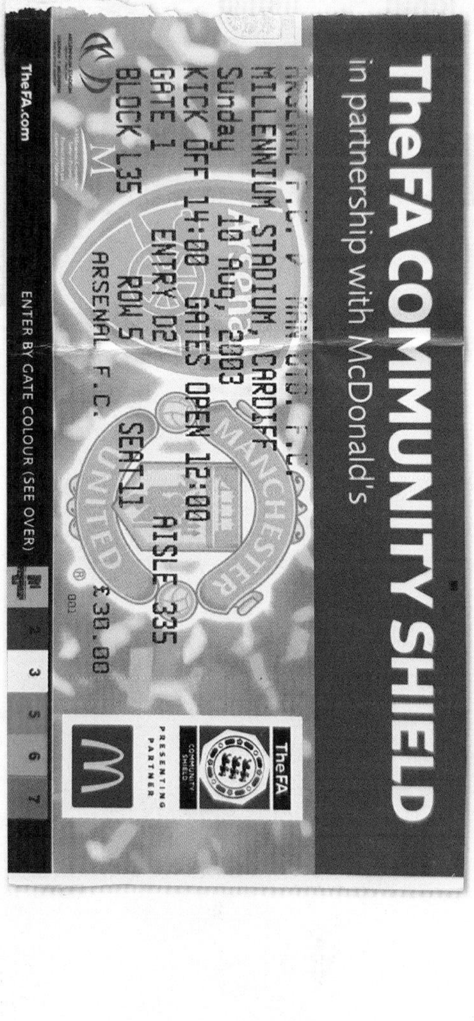
TheFA COMMUNITY SHIELD
in partnership with McDonald's
MILLENNIUM STADIUM, CARDIFF
Sunday 10 Aug, 2003
KICK OFF 14:00 GATES OPEN 12:00
GATE 1 ENTRY D2 AISLE 335
BLOCK L35 ROW 5 SEAT11 £30.00
ARSENAL F.C.
ENTER BY GATE COLOUR (SEE OVER)
TheFA.com
TheFA
PRESENTING PARTNER

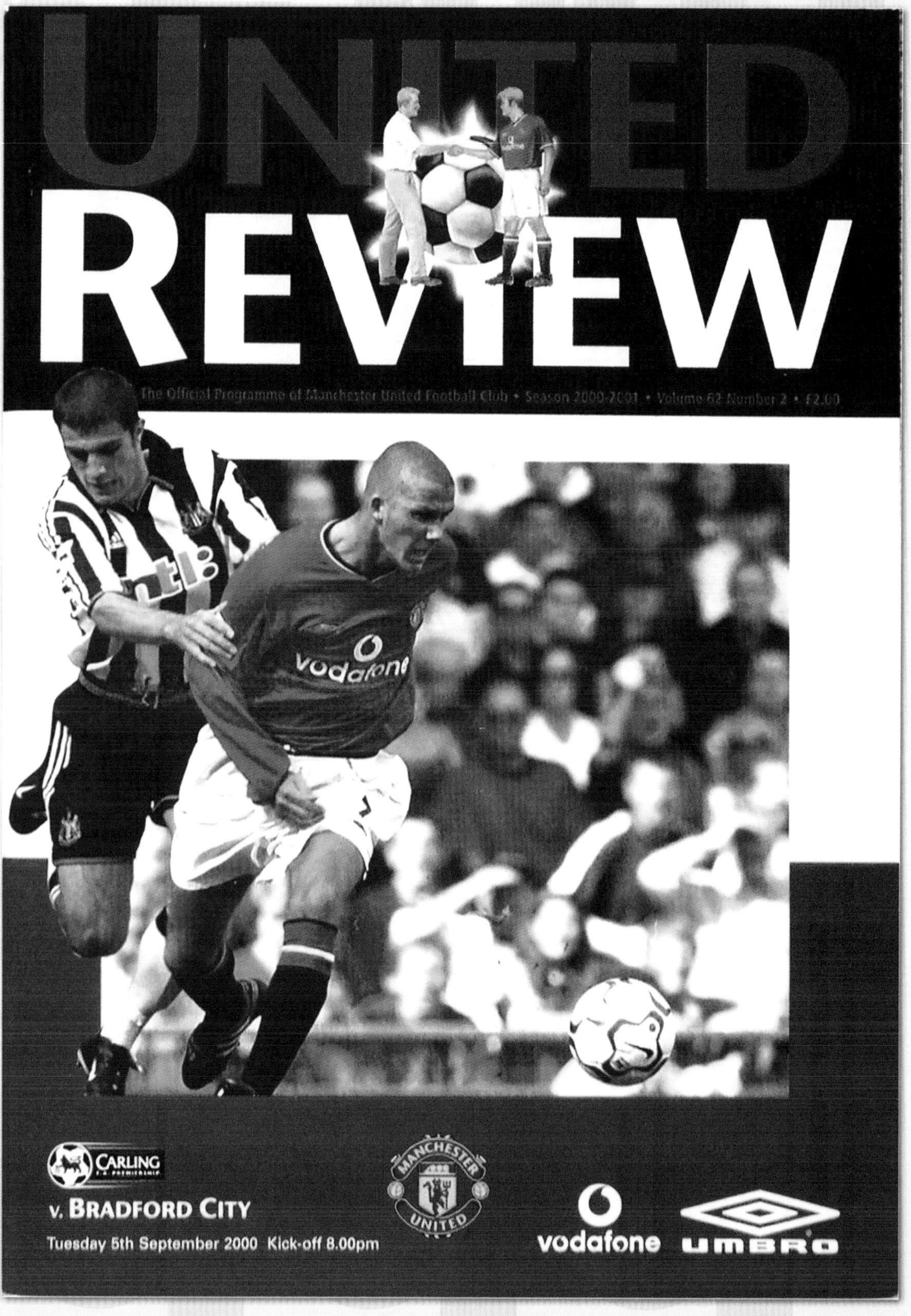
UNITED
REVIEW
The Official Programme of Manchester United Football Club • Season 2000-2001 • Volume 62 Number 2 • £2.00
vodafone
CARLING
v. BRADFORD CITY
Tuesday 5th September 2000 Kick-off 8.00pm
MANCHESTER UNITED
vodafone
UMBRO

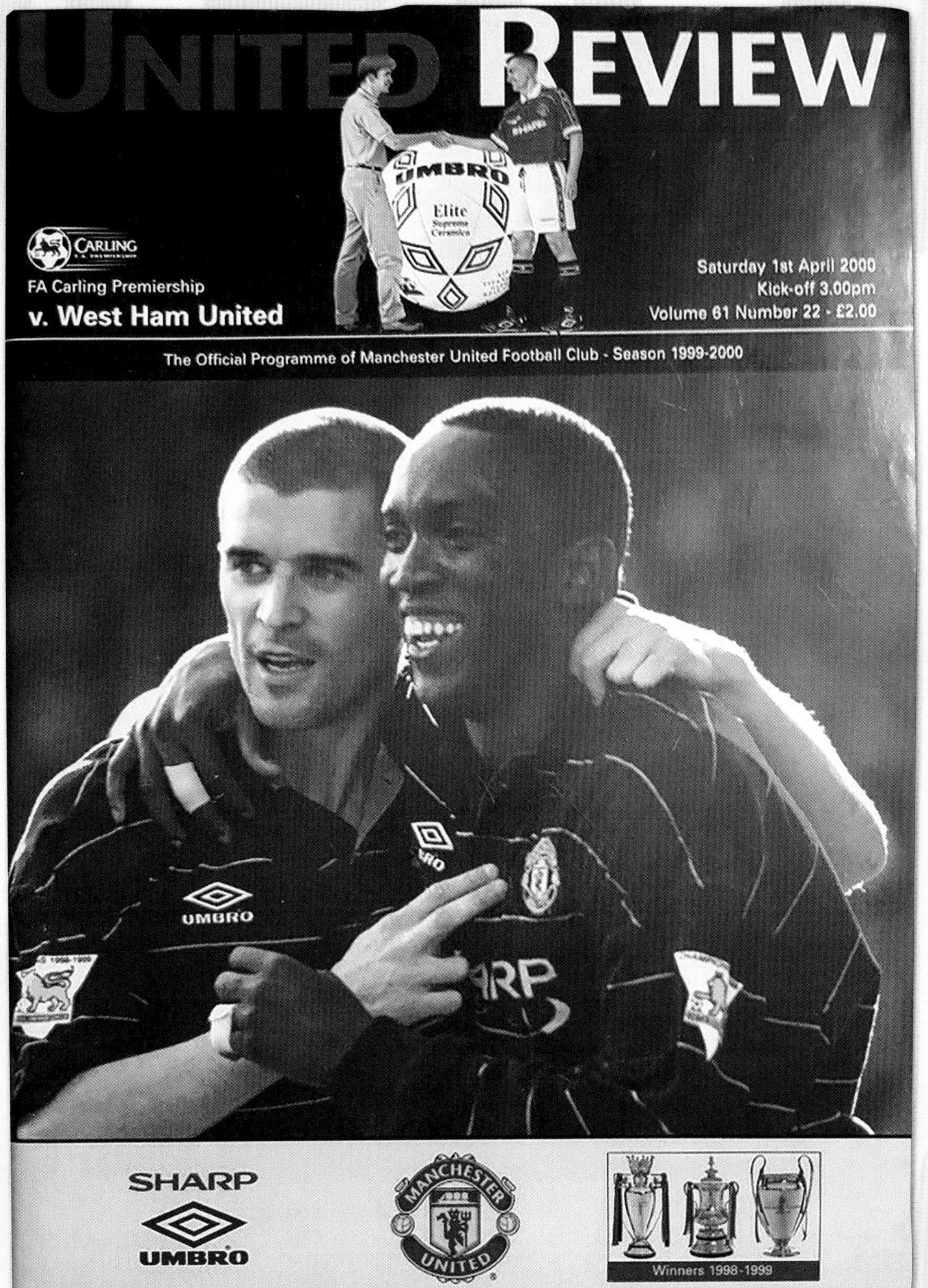
UNITED REVIEW
CARLING
FA Carling Premiership
v. West Ham United
Saturday 1st April 2000
Kick-off 3.00pm
Volume 61 Number 22 - £2.00
The Official Programme of Manchester United Football Club - Season 1999-2000
UMBRO
SHARP
UMBRO
MANCHESTER UNITED
Winners 1998-1999

2004 – A Slight Hitch

Ferguson signs Wayne Rooney but United only manage third in the League for the third successive season. In 2006, Ferguson celebrates twenty years at the club helping United to a ninth Premier League title.

Ferguson had another problem. He had failed to provide new blood for the ageing players in his side, something he had always been proud of being able to achieve. Keane was just inches away from the end of his career and other players had failed to live up to expectations. With two notable exceptions.

Wayne Rooney arrived at Old Trafford from Everton and was soon to line up alongside a new defender, the Argentinian Gabriel Heinze, for what evolved into an unyielding season that had no joy to offer in any form for the Red Devils. Fortunately, Ferguson had struck gold with these two players, unlike some of his signings of the recent past. But he was always quick to spot real talent. Rooney was only eighteen years old but had already worn the England shirt and was proving to be one of the country's best players. Defender Heinze made his debut for the club in September and it didn't take long for him to become an absolute favourite at Old Trafford; he was voted the club's best player for the 2004/05 season.

Yet the writing was on the wall as early as the 8th of August 2004 when United met perennial foes Arsenal in the Charity Shield match and were downed 3-1. The next warning came one week later in the first match in the Premiership against Chelsea. Fergie's men walked away smarting from a 1-0 defeat.

The next eleven games produced just four wins and a humiliating defeat at the hands of lowly Portsmouth, 2-0. Despite a 5-2 goal feast against Crystal Palace, United struggled to lift themselves above third place in the table, holding on to second position for six weeks before dropping back again. And there they remained whilst Arsenal took second place and Chelsea topped the table and took the title, eighteen points clear of the northerners. United went through convincingly to the FA Cup final match against Arsenal, only to lose to the London side on penalties, 4-5.

There was light in the darkness, though; Rooney and Ronaldo gelled to form a formidable partnership that indicated a bright future for them and the club. Ronaldo was a thoroughbred who needed special care and attention so that his unique talents could shine, whereas Rooney was already a finished product as his superb hat-trick in the 6-2 Champions League drubbing of Fenebahce on the 28th of September 2004 proved. His first goal was a blazing thirty-yard drive, and his overall confidence was that of a mature man; the effect this had on the weaker

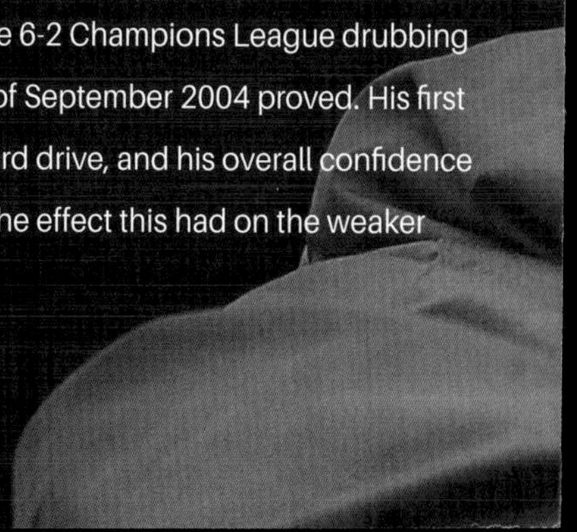

vodafone
afone

LEFT: Rooney and Ronaldo respond to Liverpool fans after Rooney scored during the Barclays Premiership match at Anfield, 15th January 2005

ABOVE: Rooney during a group D Champions League match against Sparta Prague in Prague, 19th October 2004

" You leave my players alone "

members of the squad was electric. Ferguson, ever the canny Scot, had already proven that he could handle difficult but uniquely talented players when Cantona had been at the club, and he now offered the same care bundle to Ronaldo, advising, encouraging and helping but also insisting on rest when it was appropriate. His efforts were to pay huge dividends. And Ferguson remained fiercely loyal to Roy Keane, even maintaining the 4–5–1 system so that Keane would not be forced to cover as much of the pitch as he used to do. He was now 33, not the oldest player in football, but, in fact, his time at Manchester was all but over.

For a while, it seemed that Alex Ferguson's tenure at the club might be over as well as he endured the worst months at the club since those grim days in 1989. That 2004/05 season will also go down in history books for an incident that happened off the pitch. Having ended Arsenal's forty-nine game undefeated run with a 2-0 victory, the Arsenal manager Arsene Wenger apparently accosted van Nistelrooy in the tunnel and words were exchanged. When Ferguson heard it, he rushed out of the tunnel and snapped at Wenger, *"You leave my players alone"*.

Despite being known for his outbursts of temper, Ferguson insisted that on this occasion he had kept his fireworks under control but that before he knew what had happened he was covered in pizza. The culprit was assumed to be Arsenal player Cesc Fàbregas. So began a feud between Wenger and Ferguson that lasted until 2009.

It was hard to believe that a corner had been turned for the 2005/06 season with the Magnier affair rumbling on and confirmation that Glazer was going to take over. Fergie brought in some strength for the defence and midfield in the forms of Dutch keeper Edwin van der Sar and the talented Korean Park Ji-Sung.

United started the season well, but when they only took one win from five games in September, the flak started up again, aimed in the manager's direction. Losing to Blackburn 2-1 at home incurred the wrath of the fans and the once adored manager was booed during the match. At full time he left the field with security guards and with the verbal vitriol of fans ringing in his ears. There were newspaper reports that the players were unhappy with the game tactics; that they resulted in the team losing the sharpness of former seasons. A consequence, they felt, of sticking to the, now infamous, 4-5-1 formation.

There was talk of demonstrations calling for Ferguson to go. Criticism assailed him and the assistant coach Carlos Queiroz from all quarters. The pressure rattled Ferguson, and his temper got the better of him causing him to get angry and leave a TV interview prematurely. Fergie fielded the brickbats with a somewhat more subdued defence than normal; *"... when you lose a game there is always that opportunity to recover from a defeat... we have tasted defeat in the past and it will happen again"*.

Even arch foe Arsenal manager Arsène Wenger stood up to defend the Manchester manager, condemning the fans' treatment of him, calling it *"... nearly unbelievable"*.

Defeat was to loom large in United's future. But the League season improved considerably to the point where they were in second place from late November until the end of the season. They even beat eventual winners Chelsea and third-placed Liverpool once along the way, 1-0 each time. But they couldn't make up the ground, and Chelsea finished 8 points clear on 91. Still, nine consecutive victorious games until the 29th of April 2006 when they lost 3-0 to Chelsea, was a clear warning to all comers that Ferguson had finally steadied the ship and the club was sailing towards the dawn.

In February, the League Cup was theirs after defeating Wigan Athletic 4-0. True, it was but a small peace offering, because the FA Cup challenge petered out in the face of Liverpool's 1-0 victory over them in the fifth round.

Worst of all, however, was the run in the European competition, where the Red Devils could only manage one

Sir Alex Ferguson and Arsene Wenger of Arsenal shout instructions from the sidelines during the Barclays Premiership match at Old Trafford, 17th September 2006

victory in their group, against Benfica on the 27th of September 2005 when Scholes and van Nistelrooy gave them a 2-1 victory. The fans had given the team a moment of respite and loudly got behind them. But Benfica reversed the scores in December, which meant that United had failed to reach the knockout round for the first time since the 1993/94 season. The newspapers were scathing. *"It will be interesting to see how Ferguson explains all this, because the performance tonight was as listless as the previous five in this competition"*, exclaimed one commentator.

It was a bitter blow for Ferguson.

It came on the heels of another bitter blow.

Roy Keane had been badly injured during the 0-0 draw against Liverpool; in fact, he had broken the metatarsal bone of his left foot.

Keane had become an increasingly uncomfortable thorn in Ferguson's side. Now, he was openly arguing with both management and players and let it be known in the media that once the season ended he would be *"... prepared to play elsewhere"*.

The public show of disloyalty hurt and angered the manager. Nor were the players spared, and many of them, especially Rio

> *" ... he was our leader and he left a mark...*
> *our dedication comes from the standards he set "*

Ferdinand, came in for harsh criticism. Ferguson, it seemed, had lost control of one of his favoured players and more arguments flared up between the two. Ferguson was angry. *"What you have to do as a manager is to make sure the criticism remains inside your doors. I am unremitting in that respect, totally unequivocal... you don't criticise any Manchester United players outside the doors".*

Ferguson was used to criticism aimed at him, as was every football manager. But he did not want the morale of his team affected by discontented apples in the barrel, no matter how much he respected the talent of the people involved.

The situation was untenable for club and manager. An agreement was reached, and a career at United that had spanned the years between 1993 and 2005 was ended on the 18th of November when Roy Keane left Old Trafford for the last time. It was the unhappy severance of an illustrious career. But he has been described as an *"unhappy soul"* whose last years had been marked by carping at his team mates and even the fans when he had used the unfortunate term, *"prawn sandwich brigade"* to describe them, actions that left him distanced from many of those around him. Having been suspended for the 1999 final, sadly Keane's dream of playing and winning a UEFA European Champions League final with United was to remain unrealised.

Even though he was one of those players Keane had criticised, Darren Fletcher later said of the former captain, *"... he was our leader and he left a mark... our dedication comes from the standards he set".*

Gary Neville assumed the captaincy.

In the disruption and instability that seemed to have gripped the club, compounded by injuries to several key players, even the manager's job seemed likely to be up for grabs before too long. Commentators called for his retirement but the Scot was having none of it. Questions about his future remained unanswered by him, but he made it clear that he had a job to do and that job was at United.

The increasing lack of faith in the club was infused with sadness when the incomparable Irish footballer George Best, one of the most exciting players ever to have worn a United shirt, and, indeed, of his generation, died at the age of 59. Best was probably the first of the celebrity footballers, those players whose lifestyles would later prove so irksome to Alex Ferguson.

There was trouble in another corner. Ruud van Nistelrooy had been coming into conflict with Ronaldo, irked by his tendency to hug the ball and not release it to colleagues, and van Nistelrooy was also unhappy at having been left on the bench for so many matches. Ferguson knew that he had to encourage new blood in keeping with his policy of planning ahead with the young players in mind, and one of the sacrifices made to the gods of football at the end of the season was Ruud van Nistelrooy; his career at United was over. In July, Ferguson announced that the player wanted to leave. Van Nistelrooy's legacy was five seasons with the club and a total of 150 goals in 219 appearances. And he was top goal scorer with a total of 24 goals for his final season.

The mood at Old Trafford could be summed up in this Guardian quote from July 2006; *"Almost everything about the club reeks of disarray. Owned by the Glazers, who push buttons from a remote hideaway like Dr. Evil; run by a manager who shreds his legacy at every turn; almost exclusively represented by the inadequate (Darren Fletcher and Kieran Richardson) and the odious (Rio Ferdinand); unable to close a deal for West Brom's reserve keeper, never mind the new Roy Keane. The signing of Michael Carrick... is a band aid for a bullet wound, and a ludicrously expensive one at that".*

Roy Keane celebrates with team-mates after their first goal against Leeds during their premiereship match, 30th March 2002

Ouch.

The" *Ferguson face"* was something that the manager had acquired long before, the result of advice from a friend of his about dealing with the media. Don't let your worries show in your face, his friend had told him, and Ferguson took the advice to heart. He trained himself and prepared himself mentally before interviews and experience taught him all about the tricks of the trade that journalists were employing to catch him. He eventually found out how to avoid revealing the weaknesses of his team when confronted with difficult questions without an easy answer; that could prove to be a deadly mistake. He also learned that it was better to be taciturn, and despite the intense nature of questioning, to not let your guard down and say something stupid that would be regretted later. Nonetheless, Ferguson was not about to avoid confrontation, as his seven-year wrangle with the BBC, which only ended in August of 2011, proves. The nub of that problem had to do with an attack on Ferguson's son in relation to the transfers of some United players. Eventually Ferguson relented feeling that he had made his point. There was, said Ferguson, *"... an intensity and volatility about the modern media"* that he found hard to take. He disliked the way they distorted what he told them, but he was not about to give in to them. He was far too strong a personality for that.

But what a difference a year makes.

And what a difference the maligned Michael Carrick made, too, in midfield as United entered the 2006/07 season like a steamroller, flattening Fulham in the first match of the season 5-1. Carrick, courageously wearing Keane's number 16, proved able to find his front man almost at will, firing uncannily accurate passes all over the pitch, severing opposition defences. Fergie had been vindicated against the naysayers who had questioned his judgment in buying Michael Carrick. Now they were silent.

The Scot had abandoned the search for a direct replacement for Keane; there wasn't one. Ferguson was forced to build a different centre squad and he came up trumps. Despite his failings, Carrick's presence provided the vital stability in the centre of the field that United had been lacking. With the centre secure, the magic that Rooney and Ronaldo had promised began to materialise as their performances made them joint top goal scorers with twenty-three goals each. Good news in the defence, as well. Two relatively new men were making their presence felt at the back; Patrice Evra and Nemanja Vidić. The old boys, Scholes and Giggs felt the sea change and raised their games. The statistics speak for themselves; for just two weeks in September, United were second in the table. For every other game they were on the top spot.

There was sweet revenge in the European competition when United killed Benfica 1-0 and 3-1. There followed a glorious romp against Roma, one for the fans to savour for many years.

It was the 10th of April 2007. A Tuesday. United were at home against Roma having been beaten 2-1 in the first leg of the Champions League quarter-final. That meant that there was a lot of ground to be covered by United to make up a deficit. Ferguson was confident, as usual, and gave the opinion that if United could take the chances that they created then they had a *"massive chance"*.

So, with Ferguson deciding to leave Solskjaer on the bench, the first ten minutes of the match left the home crowd extremely nervous as the Italians got into their stride. It hardly seemed as though Manchester was going to see one of the most delightful goal festivals in their history.

But that was what was about to happen.

And it began at the feet of Ronaldo, who pushed the ball on to Carrick on the thirteenth minute. Carrick had time for one touch before he drove the ball swerving towards the net from

Michael Carrick in action during the pre-season match against Porto as part of the Amsterdam Tournament, 4th August 2006

Cristiano Ronaldo scores their fifth goal during the UEFA Champions League Quarter Final second leg match against AS Roma at Old Trafford, 10th April 2007

" ... greatest night at Old Trafford "

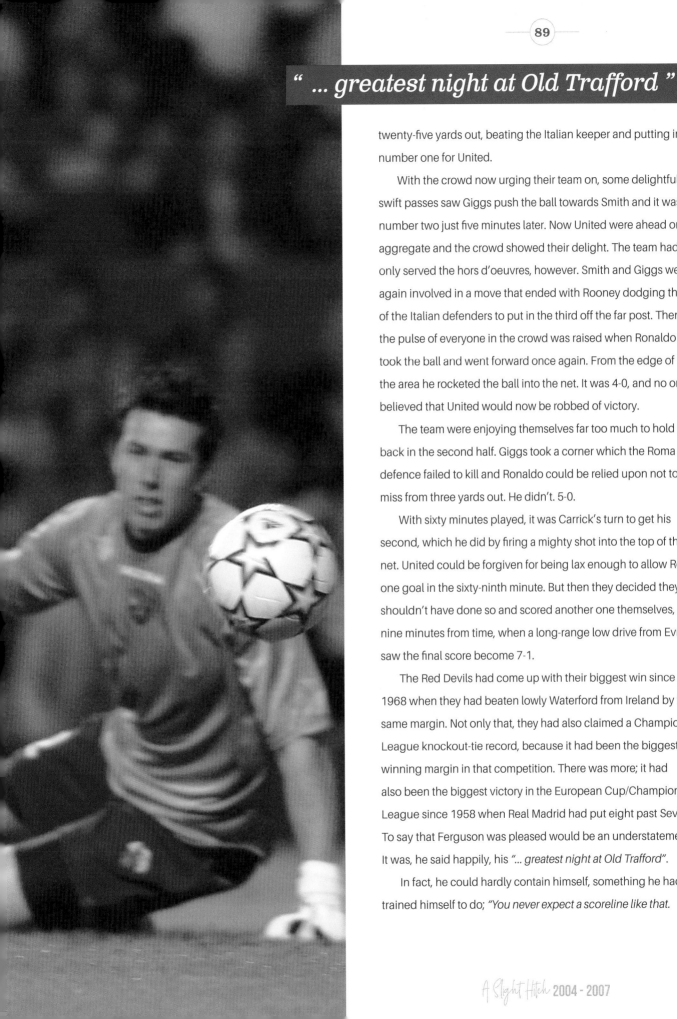

twenty-five yards out, beating the Italian keeper and putting in number one for United.

With the crowd now urging their team on, some delightful, swift passes saw Giggs push the ball towards Smith and it was number two just five minutes later. Now United were ahead on aggregate and the crowd showed their delight. The team had only served the hors d'oeuvres, however. Smith and Giggs were again involved in a move that ended with Rooney dodging three of the Italian defenders to put in the third off the far post. Then the pulse of everyone in the crowd was raised when Ronaldo took the ball and went forward once again. From the edge of the area he rocketed the ball into the net. It was 4-0, and no one believed that United would now be robbed of victory.

The team were enjoying themselves far too much to hold back in the second half. Giggs took a corner which the Roma defence failed to kill and Ronaldo could be relied upon not to miss from three yards out. He didn't. 5-0.

With sixty minutes played, it was Carrick's turn to get his second, which he did by firing a mighty shot into the top of the net. United could be forgiven for being lax enough to allow Roma one goal in the sixty-ninth minute. But then they decided they shouldn't have done so and scored another one themselves, nine minutes from time, when a long-range low drive from Evra saw the final score become 7-1.

The Red Devils had come up with their biggest win since 1968 when they had beaten lowly Waterford from Ireland by the same margin. Not only that, they had also claimed a Champions League knockout-tie record, because it had been the biggest winning margin in that competition. There was more; it had also been the biggest victory in the European Cup/Champions League since 1958 when Real Madrid had put eight past Seville. To say that Ferguson was pleased would be an understatement. It was, he said happily, his *"... greatest night at Old Trafford"*.

In fact, he could hardly contain himself, something he had trained himself to do; *"You never expect a scoreline like that.*

"Now is the time to be great"

The quality of our game was so high that... I was in the dugout thinking, 'this could be something really big here'... but certainly the number of goals and the quality of play was very, very high... the way they are playing and enjoying their football they deserve it".

But after the high, there was bitter disappointment when, having beaten Milan 3-2 at home, they were pushed out of the competition in the return leg 3-0.

But they had proven that they had the stamina and the experience to cope with the challenges, and they proved it again when they travelled to Everton on the 28th of April.

"Now is the time to be great", Ferguson encouraged his players before the game. *"Every match feels like a cup final now. I wouldn't have it any other way, because this is what it's all about, big games on the last lap of the season".*

Ronaldo was on the bench owing to an injury, and the first half did not match up to the flourish of words by the manager. Everton came out determined to fight and soon had a free kick awarded to them. Stubbs slammed the ball goalwards and when Carrick flicked out his leg, the ball was deflected past van der Sar into the United net. Everton were 1-0 in front. Worryingly, the all-important midfield was being dominated by Everton. Rooney was left alone to go for goal and with the news that Chelsea were in front in their game, Ferguson had reason to be nervous that his players were plainly struggling.

It got worse. Five minutes of the second half played and United found themselves 2-0 down. The defence had been far too slow in shutting down an Everton attack and Fernandez was given time to move the ball to his right foot and fire a shot from twenty yards into the United goal.

Then Everton seemed to lose their momentum. A defensive lapse that allowed John O'Shea an easy chance of a goal was quickly snapped up and United had pulled one back; everyone, including Ferguson was suddenly reinvigorated, with Ferguson sending Ronaldo on to do battle. The manager had gambled on the fact that Ronaldo would become the focus of Everton's defence and relieve the pressure on Giggs, Scholes and Rooney. A small insight into his strategic thinking. The effects were immediate; just seven minutes later, with pressure piling up in the Everton goalmouth, Neville fumbled his attempted clearance and put the ball into his own net.

It was O'Shea, then, with eleven minutes left to play, who floated the ball towards the Everton goal, where a deflection found the feet of Wayne Rooney, who put United ahead for the first time in the match.

Everton failed to retake the initiative; fatal when the Red Devils were now resurgent. Chances came and went for United and it seemed unlikely that Everton would score again. As the final minutes ticked away, Ronaldo saw Chris Eagles sprinting into a gap in the Everton defence and despite almost losing his footing, Eagles recovered his equilibrium, picked up Ronaldo's through pass and curled the ball into the net. 4-2.

Ferguson confessed to being slightly baffled by what had happened in the game, which at one point seemed to have been out of United's control. The best that he could come up with was, *"... it was meant to be".*

Despite two draws and two losses in the final seven games of the season, United went on to take the Premiership title with 89 points to Chelsea's 83.

And hopes were high when United walked out for the FA Cup final against Chelsea, hopes that the Double would make the season even sweeter. Those hopes were dashed, as Chelsea lifted the trophy with a 1-0 victory after extra time.

The personal awards handed out that year confirmed the dominant form of individual United players; eight players were named in the PFA Team of the Year; Van der Saar, Neville, Evra, Vidić, Ferdinand, Scholes, Giggs, Ronaldo. An enormous compliment to Ferguson's skill at spotting talent. There were still some voices that wanted to prick the balloon, however, but Ferguson brushed off suggestions that he should retire by

Wayne Rooney celebrates after scoring against Everton during their Premiership football match at Goodison Park, 28th April 2007

" Fear has to come into it, but you can be too hard "

countering, *"It's none of their business... it disgusts me that people think that way"*.

Having already picked up the World Manager of the Year award for 2007, he received another compliment when he won the Manager of the Season award. Cristiano Ronaldo received eight individual awards for his performances. That season he had scored United's 2000th goal with Ferguson as manager, when United had beaten Aston Villa 3-0 on the 23rd of December 2006.

There were even more reasons why the year had been memorable; Fergie had celebrated twenty years at the club in November 2006, a period summed up by Sir Bobby Charlton; *"He has given Manchester United the most fantastic ride... it has never been boring... he has made Manchester United what we always thought it was - number one"*.

And the BBC highlighted what was going on in the world in 1986 when the Scot arrived in Manchester. *"It was the year of Chernobyl, the NASA Challenger disaster, and Margaret Thatcher was in the seventh of her eleven years as PM. The 1986 World Cup in Mexico saw Maradona's infamous Hand of God, while closer to home, Steaua Bucuresti had won the European Cup and Oxford the League Cup. And Sarah Ferguson married Prince Andrew"*.

Ferguson had developed the reputation of being a dictator, ferocious in his demands. *"Fear has to come into it, but you can be too hard"*, he said. *"If players are fearful all the time, they won't perform well, either. But I had to lift players' expectations. They should never give in. I said that to them all the time: 'If you give in once, you'll give in twice.' And the work ethic and energy I had seemed to spread throughout the club"*.

That season also saw a charity football match to mark the memorable occasion when the Busby Babes entered European football.

Quite a year.

Ferguson congratulates Alan Smith as they celebrate winning the Premiership title at the end of the match against West Ham at Old Trafford, 13th May 2007

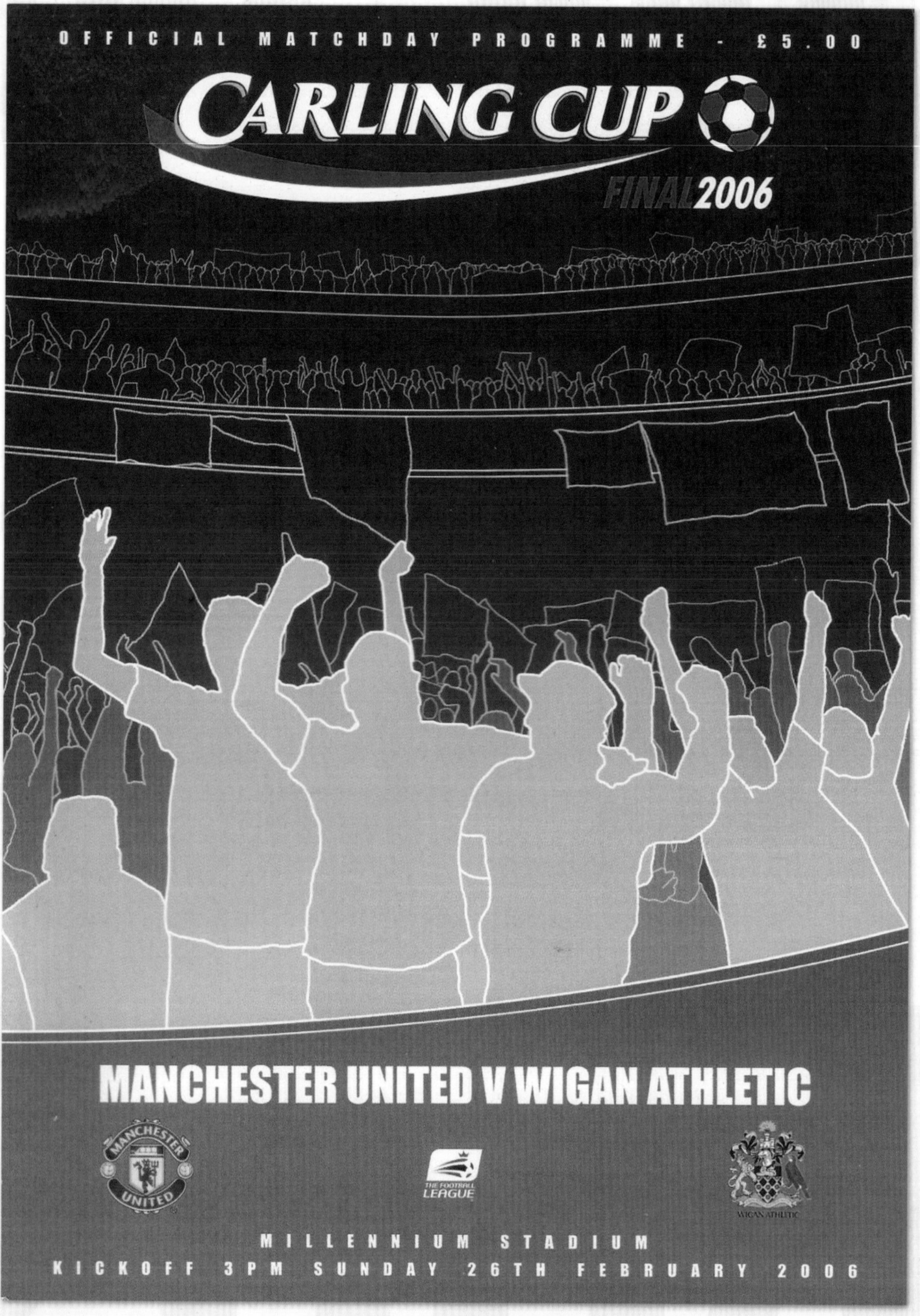
OFFICIAL MATCHDAY PROGRAMME - £5.00
CARLING CUP
FINAL 2006
MANCHESTER UNITED V WIGAN ATHLETIC
MANCHESTER UNITED
THE FOOTBALL LEAGUE
WIGAN ATHLETIC
MILLENNIUM STADIUM
KICKOFF 3PM SUNDAY 26TH FEBRUARY 2006

The FA CUP
e·on
CHELSEA v
MANCHESTER UNITED
THE FA CUP SPONSORED BY E.ON
2007 FINAL
OFFICIAL MATCHDAY PROGRAMME £10
SATURDAY 19 MAY 2007 3.00pm
WEMBLEY STADIUM
WEMBLEY STADIUM

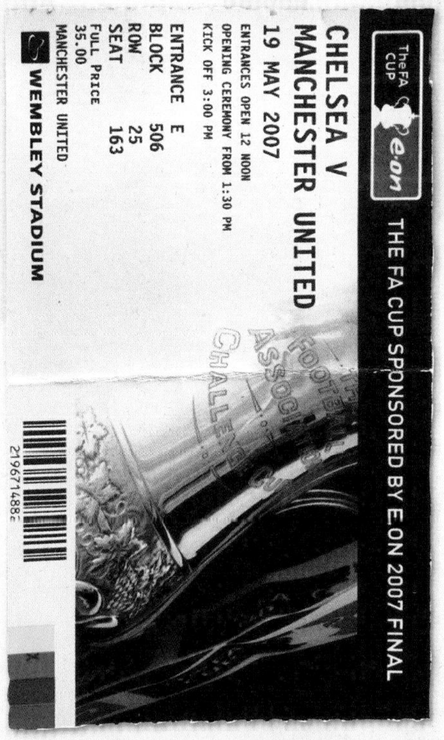
The FA CUP
e·on
THE FA CUP SPONSORED BY E.ON 2007 FINAL
CHELSEA V
MANCHESTER UNITED
19 MAY 2007
ENTRANCES OPEN 12 NOON
OPENING CEREMONY FROM 1:30 PM
KICK OFF 3:00 PM
ENTRANCE E
BLOCK 506
ROW 25
SEAT 163
FULL PRICE
35.00
MANCHESTER UNITED
WEMBLEY STADIUM

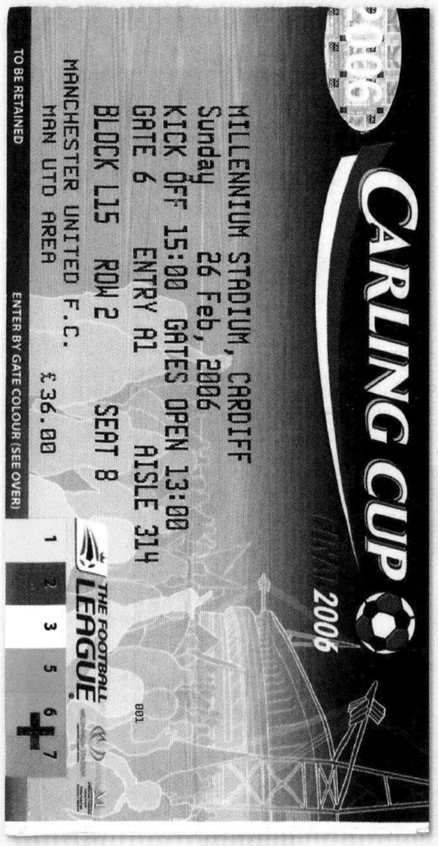
CARLING CUP
2006
MILLENNIUM STADIUM, CARDIFF
Sunday 26 Feb, 2006
KICK OFF 15:00 GATES OPEN 13:00
GATE 6 ENTRY A1 AISLE 314
BLOCK L15 ROW 2 SEAT 8
MANCHESTER UNITED F.C.
MAN UTD AREA £ 36.00
TO BE RETAINED
ENTER BY GATE COLOUR (SEE OVER)
THE FOOTBALL LEAGUE

2007 The Records Fall

Ferguson declares the team to be the best squad he has ever assembled. He brings home his second European Cup. On the 19th December 2010, Ferguson became Manchester United's longest-serving manager, overtaking Matt Busby's record of twenty-four years, one month and thirteen days in charge of the club. Charges of improper conduct are made. Ferguson wins his twelfth and Manchester United's nineteenth league title and the team beats Liverpool's record of eighteen.

But Ferguson had only just begun. The 2006/07 season had been just the warm-up act. Not for the first time in his career, Ferguson was about to prove the doubters had been too quick to bring out the knives. He had bought Owen Hargreaves from Bayern Munich to make the midfield even more difficult for opposition teams, Luís Carlos Almeida da Cunha, the Portuguese winger known as Nani, and Brazilian midfielder Anderson Luís de Abreu Oliveira, to show that he meant business. With the latter two players he was remaining true to his philosophy of bringing on younger players to replace those in the first team who might only have a few more years in the side. Indeed, Ole Gunnar Solskjaer gave Ferguson a timely reminder when he retired in August 2008.

The following season of 2007/08 was a cliffhanger, but there was a buzz of anticipation in the air at Old Trafford, and any of the fans who stayed the course were treated to a sizzling United side, burning to bring home the trophies.

Not that it seemed that way when they drew the first two matches and lost the third to Manchester City 1-0. They swiftly recovered, however, and remained undefeated for the next ten matches, bouncing around between first and second place in the table. Ferguson declared his confidence in the team and right enough, by the middle of March 2008, they had cemented their lead at the top. Despite a wobble when they lost 2-1 to rivals Chelsea, they survived the fright and took their tenth Premiership title two points clear on eighty-five points.

Ryan Giggs had now surpassed Sir Bobby Charlton's 758 appearances in the red shirt. In seven games United had thundered home four goals and they thrashed Newcastle United 6-0 and 5-1 for good measure, just in case there were any outstanding revenge issues. Whizzkid Ronaldo put

2011

Carlos Tevez in action during the UEFA Champions League Final match against Chelsea at the Luzhniki Stadium in Moscow, 21st May 2008

" ... if this team goes on now and wins the European Cup, it will be my best ever "

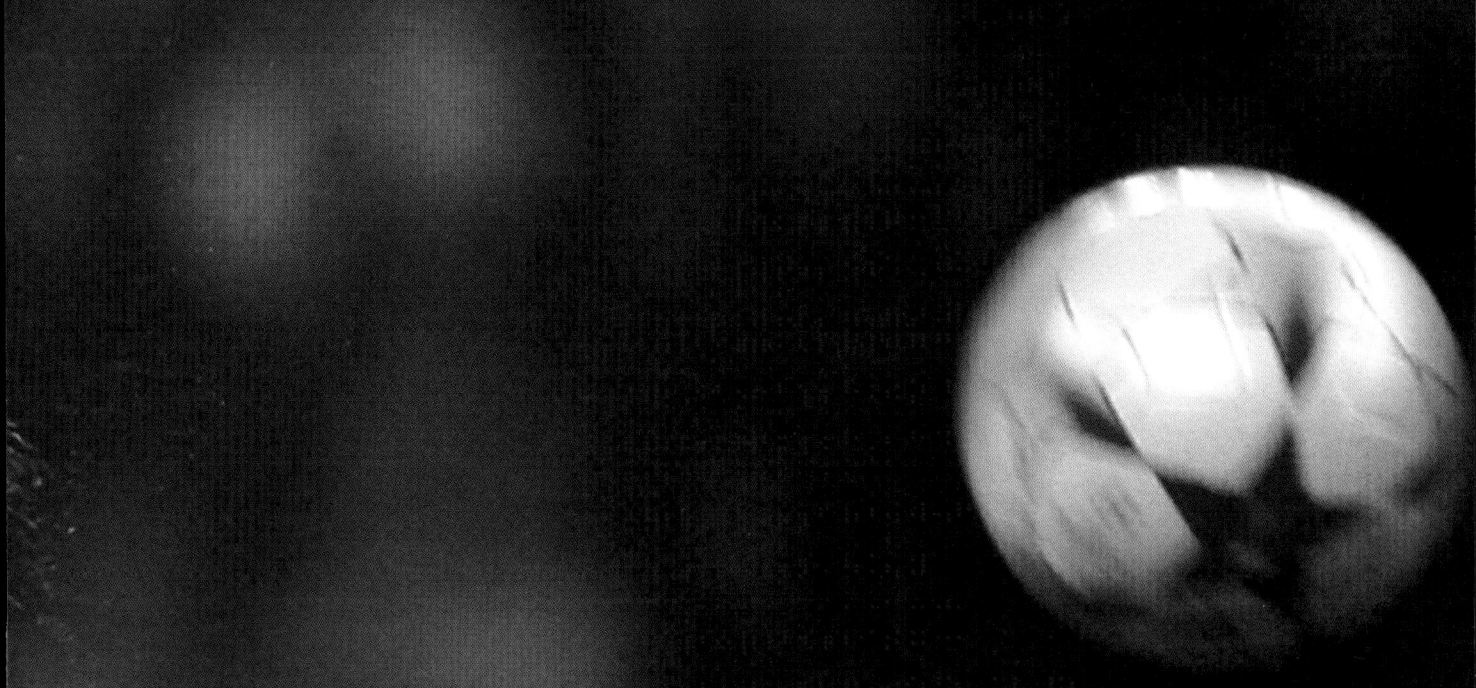

an astonishing forty-two goals in total into the opposition nets, thirty-one of those in the League, which earned him the Premier League Golden Boot to go with the five other awards he earned that season.

"The Premier League is so competitive you can't ease up for a minute and it can be difficult picking your teams if you are going for the League as well as Europe", Ferguson told the media.

It wasn't all milk and honey though; United were ignominiously dumped out of the League Cup by Coventry, 2-0, and Portsmouth did the honours in the FA Cup, 1-0 in round six – an unfortunate debut for Carlos Tevez – both matches in front of a home crowd.

But in Europe, it was a different story altogether and Ronaldo was the sole saviour on two occasions as United chopped their way past Roma and Barcelona to meet Chelsea in the final. Ferguson had announced that *"... if this team goes on now and wins the European Cup, it will be my best ever... we're alive and kicking and can't wait to take on Chelsea"*.

In Ferguson's opinion, the European final was now even more important than the World Cup and as such was top priority for every European manager. Not least because in 2008, the financial incentive for the two finalists would be to share out perhaps half of the two hundred and ten million pounds that the competition would bring in. Rather important indeed.

Anyone who had fingernails at the beginning of the match certainly didn't have them at the end.

The match began with both sides testing their opponent's weaknesses. Ferguson had his iron men in the middle, Scholes, Hargreaves and Carrick, to counter the Chelsea midfielders, but there wasn't much to shout about until the twenty-sixth minute when Ronaldo sailed up, ten yards out, to put United ahead. The game livened up immediately with Chelsea unleashing waves of attacks that

EDWIN
VAN DER SA

LEFT: Edwin Van Der Sar celebrates winning the UEFA Champions League Final match against Chelsea at Luzhniki Stadium in Moscow, 21st May 2008

ABOVE: Nani and Cristiano Ronaldo with the Champions League trophy at Luzhniki Stadium in Moscow, 21st May 2008

almost brought the equaliser, and the excitement built as the forwards of both sides unleashed their shots goalwards. The match flowed from end to end.

And then, just before half time, the ball fell to Lampard, who slotted in the equaliser.

Chelsea took the game to United after the break and there were some lucky escapes for the Manchester side. Before the end, Drogba received his marching orders but still neither side could get the winning goal. The penalty shoot-out began.

And when it ended, United were champions of Europe, 6-5, and had achieved the European treble. What greater tribute could Ferguson and his team have paid to Matt Busby's boys who were on that fateful aircraft fifty years before that had crashed at Munich airport. *"It was such an emotional occasion... we had a cause and people with causes are difficult to play against. I think fate was playing its hand today"*, he said after the match, understandably overwrought by the enormity of the occasion.

Ten Premier League titles and now a second Champions League trophy to go alongside them.

But the end of a match is always the beginning of the next one, because that vital interlude is all that stands between success and failure. And failure was not a word that possibly the most extraordinary manager in English football history liked one little bit.

Ferguson was now confident that Liverpool's record of eighteen league titles would be overtaken by Manchester United. Not, he declared, that he was bothered about records, but he knew the game was about championships and trophies and he was certain that his young side would go on to achieve great things.

One indication that he was right came in December 2008. Having won the Champions League the previous season, United were entitled to participate in the FIFA Club World Cup challenge against five other challengers.

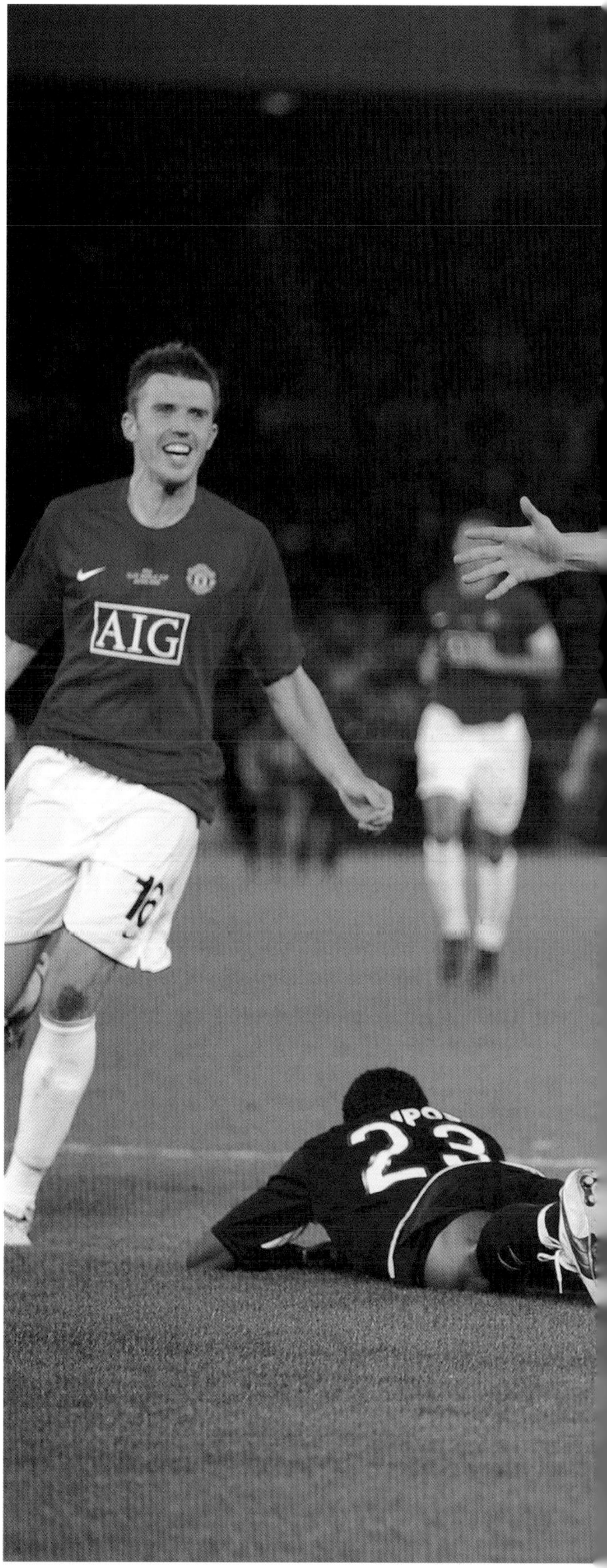

Cristiano Ronaldo congratulates Wayne Rooney during the FIFA Club World Cup Japan 2008 Final match against Liga De Quito at the International Stadium Yokohama, Kanagawa, Japan, 21st December 2008

Edwin van der Sar and Gary Neville celebrate after victory over CSKA Moscow in Moscow, 21st October 2009

They entered the competition in the semi-final stage. They dispensed with Gamba Osaka 5-3 and met up with LDU Quito in the final on December 21st, 2008.

The Red Devils got into their stride early in the game with Tevez, Rooney and Ronaldo joining forces at the front but unable to convert the chances into goals. The Ecuadorian side was unlucky not to score, before United ramped up the pressure with Rooney keen to get on the score sheet.

And then disaster struck in the second half when Vidić elbowed Claudio Bieler and was sent off. Ferguson rearranged the side, taking Tevez off and putting Evans on to bolster the defence. To everyone's relief, Rooney's persistence finally paid off in the seventy-second minute when Ronaldo laid on a pass for Rooney's low drive across goal that beat the Ecuadorian keeper. And that was the score at full-time, 1-0. It was the first time an English club had won the title.

Ferguson, who might have been tempted to regard the FIFA Club World Cup competition as somewhat of a sideshow, wholeheartedly embraced the opportunity to gain another title and be rewarded with the title Champions of the World. United under Ferguson had, indeed, come a long way from the dark days of 1989. The manager was fulsome in his praise for his team saying that they had done something very special that day. With only ten men on the field they had, he said, drawn together as a team. They had supported one another, subordinating individual brilliance to the service of the club.

This Premiership season, it would be Ferguson's nemesis Liverpool that would cause him the greatest headache. Twice they struck, 2-1 in the first match, then demolishing United 4-1 in the second.

New signing Dimitar Berbatov made his debut in that first match against Liverpool. Although a talented and elegant player, Berbatov disappointed the fans and in their opinion did not live up to the manager's claim that he was *"... A key signing... one of the best and most exciting strikers in world football... I'm sure he will be a popular player with the fans"*. He certainly wasn't. Oh well, another of those occasional Fergie moments.

It was fortunate that United had gathered enough points to stay in first place after the second Liverpool match because they promptly lost the following match against Fulham, too, 1-0. But all told it was a successful season with just four games lost and a sixteen-game unbeaten run that took them up to the middle of March 2009. They put five goals in each game past Stoke City, West Bromwich Albion, and Tottenham Hotspur in the League and Blackburn Rovers in the League Cup, with the dream team of Ronaldo and Rooney claiming forty-six goals between them by the season's end. An unbeaten run of nine games saw United go 4 points clear of Liverpool, 90 to 86, to become Premier champions once again. It was United's third consecutive league title. Now they had equalled Liverpool's eighteen. Twenty-two matches had been played without a goal being scored against them, fourteen clean sheets in successive games, a record-breaking achievement that made Ferguson eulogise about his defensive line up saying that he was *"proud of them"*. United goalkeeper Edwin van der Sar soon held the British record for clean sheets.

They almost sauntered through the League Cup competition and rightfully won the cup in March although Tottenham made them struggle for it and United could only claim the prize after winning 4-1 on penalties.

There were disturbing tendencies in the European competition, however, with four drawn games and only two victories; enough, nonetheless, to put United at the top of their group and perhaps dispel the niggling quibbles. These were firmly put to bed in the knockout stage when Porto and Arsenal were put out to pasture.

Ferguson was excited; he could almost smell the glory in becoming the first manager of the first team to retain the Champions League title. The Red Devils had just one hurdle left to clear; Barcelona.

United got off to a good start in the final, putting enormous pressure on the Spaniards with Ronaldo coming dangerously close to scoring, but it was a brief moment of light that died after ten minutes when the Catalans' first attempt at goal succeeded.

Barcelona's flowing passing always remained dangerous to the English team and as the first half moved to its close, the Spanish team grew in confidence with Lionel Messi causing all manner of problems in the United defence. Ferguson changed the formation to 4-2-2 for the second half and added Tevez to fight alongside Ronaldo.

Barcelona started out in fighting form in the second half

“ ...eighty million pounds for Cristiano Ronaldo... ”

and came dangerously close to the English goal. Again, the accurate passing by the Spaniards contrasted strongly with the sometimes sloppy English version. And then suddenly, United recovered their good form of the first minutes of the match. Short-lived hope flickered but that flame faded, too, and as the sixty-sixth minute approached, Ferguson decided action was needed and he brought on Berbatov to replace Park. United were now going forward in search of the goal but that left them dangerously exposed at the back, and the gaps were exploited by the Catalan team. Before much more time had passed, Lionel Messi had sent a header into the net for Barcelona’s second.

There were twenty minutes to go. In a desperate last move to try and avert almost certain defeat, Ferguson sent on Paul Scholes who replaced Ryan Giggs and took over the captaincy. It did nothing to change the result and when the whistle sounded, United’s challenge was over. Barcelona’s easy passing skills had rendered United ineffective, and even Alex Ferguson, distraught at the defeat of his team, feeling that his boys had played below their best, was forced to admit that the best team had won. *“At times, Barcelona can make you look silly because they keep the ball so well. At times we maybe chased it and didn’t keep our shape as well as we should have”.*

So near and yet so far. Just like the League Cup, which had slipped from their grasp in the semi-final against Everton, where yet another penalty shootout had decided the game, this time in Everton’s favour, 2-4.

Nonetheless, United had claimed three trophies, four including the Community Shield, which they had won against Portsmouth in August, 3-1, after a penalty shoot-out. United seemed to be making a habit of getting entangled in these sudden-death moments. Not a method of winning to be wished for or relied upon.

So; dejected as manager and team might have been, certainly a sign of the high standards they had set themselves over the years, it had been a magnificent achievement by anybody’s standards. They had, after all, become the first team ever to take three top English titles consecutively on two separate occasions, the last time having been between 1999 and 2001. But it seemed as though Hermes and Heracles, those ancient Greek gods of sport, had decided that United had now had more than their fair share of glory and wanted to bring them back down to the level of ordinary mortals.

But ordinary was not where at least one of the United players wanted to be.

There was a reason for the manager to be more dejected than he might normally have been in such a situation. The bombshell came on the 11th of June; *“Manchester United have received a world record unconditional offer from Real Madrid of eighty million pounds for Cristiano Ronaldo... United have agreed to give Real Madrid permission to talk to the player”.*

Ferguson said later that Ronaldo *“... fervently wants to leave”*, and his reply was that he would consider it.

Less than one month later Ronaldo was gone.

He was such an exceptional player that there can be no doubt that his departure worried the United manager. Ronaldo commented later that he missed the relationship with Ferguson at United. Ferguson, he said, was his *“father in football”*, a man who was *“... a fantastic person. A human person”*, a tough man, but one who had taught him so many things and he had wished that the Scot could continue to be his *“life coach”*.

Cristiano Ronaldo during the Premier League match against West Bromwich Albion at The Hawthorns, 27th January 2009

Michael Owen celebrates after scoring the winning goal to make it 4-1, 20th September 2009

Ronaldo's exceptional abilities had drawn out the best qualities and great understanding from Ferguson, who was always prepared, within certain parameters that he set for himself, to grant uniquely talented players large amounts of leeway that he would not have granted to others.

United did have a pretender to Ronaldo's throne in Wayne Rooney, but only time would tell if he was he really the right man for the job.

Perhaps Carlos Tevez, too, sensed that change was about to descend on United, for he decided not to renew the terms of his loan to United and later signed to arch rivals Manchester City. He felt that he had been underused and undervalued at United and Ferguson's subsequent remarks about him, i.e. that Tevez was not worth his transfer fee, seem to confirm that Tevez was right.

Ferguson might play down the importance of this loss, but it became all too apparent that Tevez had also left a gap in the field that the manager subsequently failed to replace; at great cost. The manager defended himself by saying *"I'm not the slightest bit worried. It happens and you can't keep all of the players all of the time"*.

The fans were worried, nonetheless, and in no doubt about the value of a Carlos Tevez, and when he scored twenty-nine for Manchester City that season, they knew they had been right and the manager wrong. And they were not alone in their opinion in the football world. No one is immune from obstinacy.

Ferguson's eye fell on the ex-Newcastle United player Michael Owen, whose contract with Newcastle had expired, and he came to Old Trafford for a three-year spell. Owen did well; Ronaldo he was not.

Put bluntly, the season unravelled and led to disappointment all round. Some disappointment might have been expected after such a glorious 2008/09 season, but lifting just one trophy, the League Cup, had not been in anybody's forecast, least of all Ferguson's. The club had been chasing a record-breaking nineteenth League title to trump Liverpool's eighteen, so hopes were high. But now those key player absences were sorely felt and they had unbalanced the side.

Although United did well in the Premiership and almost made it to the title, six defeats, two of them against Chelsea, 0-1 and 1-2 proved to be their undoing and it was Chelsea who took the top spot by one point, 86 to 85. Doubly galling as Chelsea had also taken the Community Shield game in August 2009, 4-1 on penalties. The team members were still working well together; Wigan were downed twice 5-0, and there were six games when they netted four goals in each match; the most satisfying occasion was when United played the lads from the other side of town, Manchester City.

In that match, Tevez proved his worth to United's opponents, who were without their star signings Robinho and Adebeyor, but it was still the Red Devils who were in front within two minutes with Rooney doing the honours. An exciting game got underway and the chances came and went at both ends but despite United's slight midfield advantage a bad mistake saw City's Barry score the equaliser when Tevez seized on the opportunity to take the ball from United's keeper Ben Foster, who was outside of the box, and pass to his teammate. A sloppy Rooney pass almost allowed City to go into the lead, with only the goalpost preventing a 2-1 deficit. And that wasn't the only close shave United had despite going on the offensive.

But after the break, United roared back into the game and a superb Ryan Giggs cross found Darren Fletcher, who headed home the second goal. In the fifty-second minute, City's Bellamy, picking up a pass from Tevez, cannoned his shot into the top right-hand corner of the United net. United had thrown away their lead again.

United recovered, got hold of the game, and the City goalkeeper was forced to keep the red wave out. Yet

" ... probably made it the best derby of all time "

with only twelve minutes left the scores were still equal. Ferguson decided that he had to act as he saw the game points slipping away. Berbatov was taken off and Michael Owen brought on in his stead.

It was Ryan Giggs once more, whose free-kick floated above the City defence to find Darren Fletcher for United's third goal. And that seemed to be that.

Except that it wasn't quite. In the final minute of time Ferdinand, for some unfathomable reason, tried to pass the ball back to the keeper almost from the halfway line. Bellamy hurtled forward and United had given away their lead for the third time. They were saved by the length of stoppage time added. Heading into the fifth minute, it was that man Giggs once again who pushed the ball through to Owen and the substitute saved United's blushes by adding a fourth goal.

The final result was 4-3 to United, but Ferguson had been rattled by the closeness of the match even though he said the goals and United's failures *"... probably made it the best derby of all time"*.

United's winner by Owen had Ferguson jumping in the air, but it was a release of tension that belied the irritation he felt. After the match he let rip; *"We made horrendous mistakes... and it kept them in the game"*, he said, blaming mistakes by Rio Ferdinand and Ben Foster for two of the City goals before then saying his side could have scored six or seven goals. Ignoring the fact that City might well have said the same. His outburst showed that he was obviously aware of problems in the team that needed repair and that was making him uneasy. He, too, can hardly have failed to notice that whenever Rooney had been injured and unable to play, the team had suffered. Possibly the old saying about putting all your eggs in one basket entered his mind.

Elsewhere, United's edge had blunted just enough to deny them victory almost every time it really mattered.

Wayne Rooney clashes with Kolo Toure during the Premier League match against Manchester City at Old Trafford, 20th September 2009

Paul Scholes applauds fans after being substituted during his own Testimonial match against New York Cosmos at Old Trafford, 5th August 2011

" It is rubbish! There is no truth in it – I have no intention of retiring "

Perhaps this was nowhere more apparent than in the FA Cup competition, which Manchester United entered in the third round. Their opponents were Leeds United, forty-three places below Manchester United in the English leagues. The League Cup final was coming up in only a short time; Ferguson opted for a blend of youth and experience. United's challenge was over after nineteen minutes when Lee scored. Bowen had missed from close range, two penalty appeals had been turned down. The gods had turned away from their erstwhile favourites. The one glow to recall times past was the League Cup victory against Aston Villa in February when Owen and Rooney secured a 2-1 victory with, Fergie confessed, a little help from the referee, who did not send Vidić off despite his foul in the penalty area.

In the UEFA Cup, United came up against stiff opposition; Bayern Munich. Ferguson was unbowed. *"There's an impressive maturity about the team in Europe nowadays... it's easy for them now".*

An early goal for United seemed to prove him right. But any slackness against a team of the calibre of Bayern is heavily punished and United were. They lost the first leg 2-1.

In the second leg, they came within a whisker of winning their quarter-final battle, but when Rafael was dismissed, Ferguson was forced to play a defensive game. The Red Devils finally lost out when Bayern went through on away goals advantage with the final score at 3-2 in United's favour. Another Ferguson outburst followed the match, but it stemmed more from frustration and deep disappointment than calm thinking. *"Typical Germans..! I don't think the best team got through... we have had occasions when we have had luck and I think they have this time. It's hard to digest. In one way we could say we have thrown it away..."* And so on.

As writer Frank Worrall pointed out, the German club's manager was Dutch and of the two of the players Ferguson aimed his ire at, one was French and the other was also Dutch.

Ferguson could have been forgiven for dreading another of those dark ages he had already experienced. Others were already having the same sensations of déjà vu.

"It is rubbish! There is no truth in it – I have no intention of retiring".

That was Ferguson when the rumours began circulating in April 2010. There was, perhaps, one vital reason why he did not want to retire just then, even though the thought must have passed through his mind often during that *"unsuccessful"* year – the League Cup really being considered to be not much above the Community Shield in status. He desperately wanted to claim that record-breaking nineteenth League title and depose Liverpool. That desire and the eternally circulating lure of the Champions League meant that for the time being, Ferguson was going nowhere.

Like Edwin van der Sar, Paul Scholes retired at the end of the season and thought his United life was over, but by the beginning of the new year he had to come back to bolster the injury-plagued side and almost helped to pull the iron out of the fire.

But only almost.

UEFA
CHAMPIONS
LEAGUE
FINAL
MOSCOW 2008
UEFA CHAMPIONS LEAGUE FINAL
MOSCOW 2008
FINAL
MANCHESTER UNITED
Luzhniki Stadium
21 May - 22:45
CHELSEA FOOTBALL CLUB
OFFICIAL PROGRAMME
260 рублей
£5.00

8.00 EURO

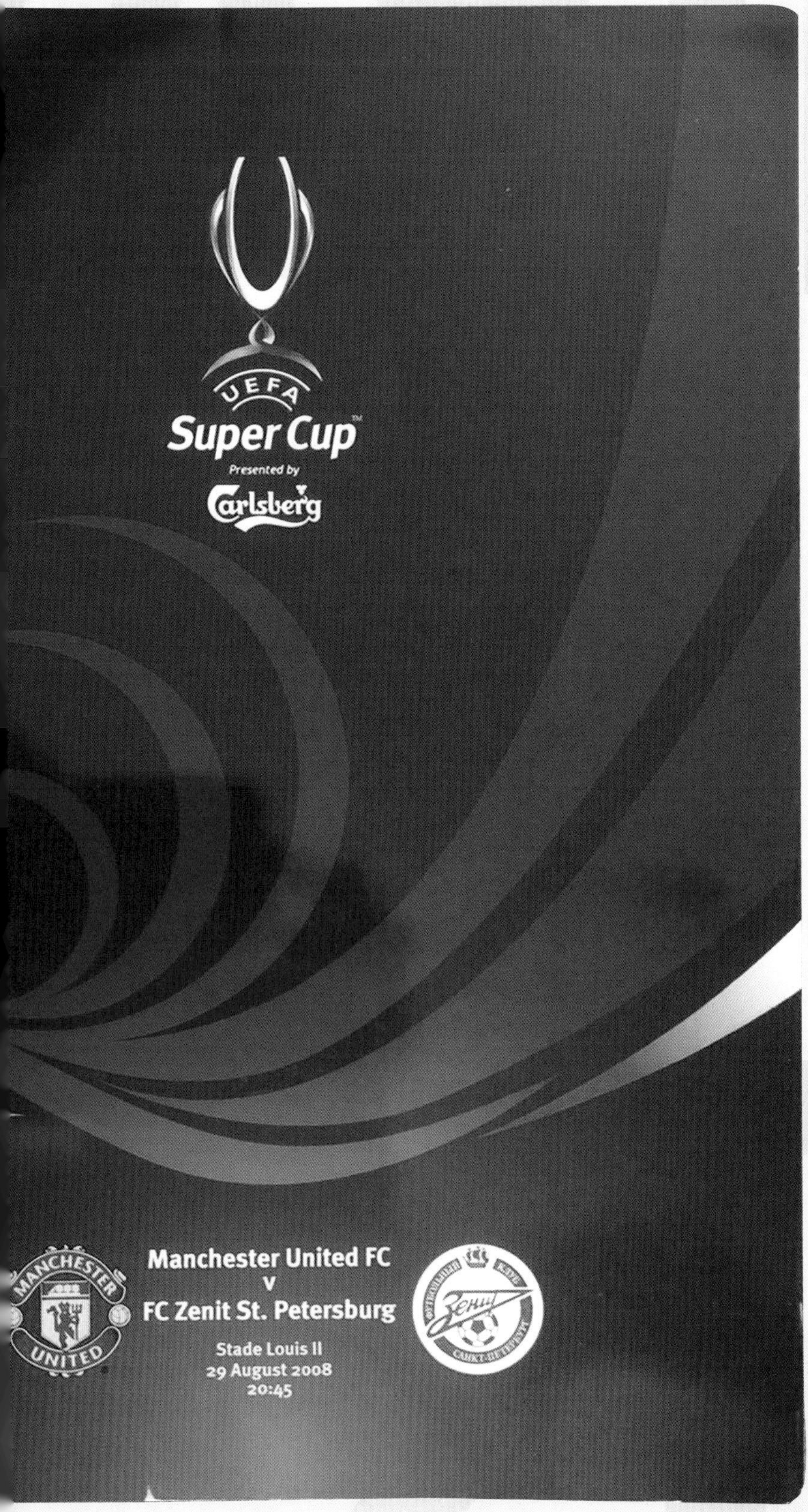
UEFA
Super Cup
Presented by
Carlsberg
Manchester United FC
v
FC Zenit St. Petersburg
Stade Louis II
29 August 2008
20:45

Luzhniki Stadium, 21 May 2008
22:45 Local Time
Tribune: D Row: 68
Section: 5 Seat: 47
Price/Цена: 140 € / 5180 руб
Chelsea FC
FINAL
MOSCOW 2008
unitegainstracism

THE FOOTBALL LEAGUE
WEMBLEY STADIUM
CARLING CUP FINAL 2009
Manchester United
v
Tottenham Hotspur
THE OFFICIAL MATCHDAY PROGRAMME £6
1ST MARCH 2009
3PM KICK OFF
WEMBLEY STADIUM
MANCHESTER UNITED
TOTTENHAM HOTSPUR

£9 €10
UEFA
CLUBS

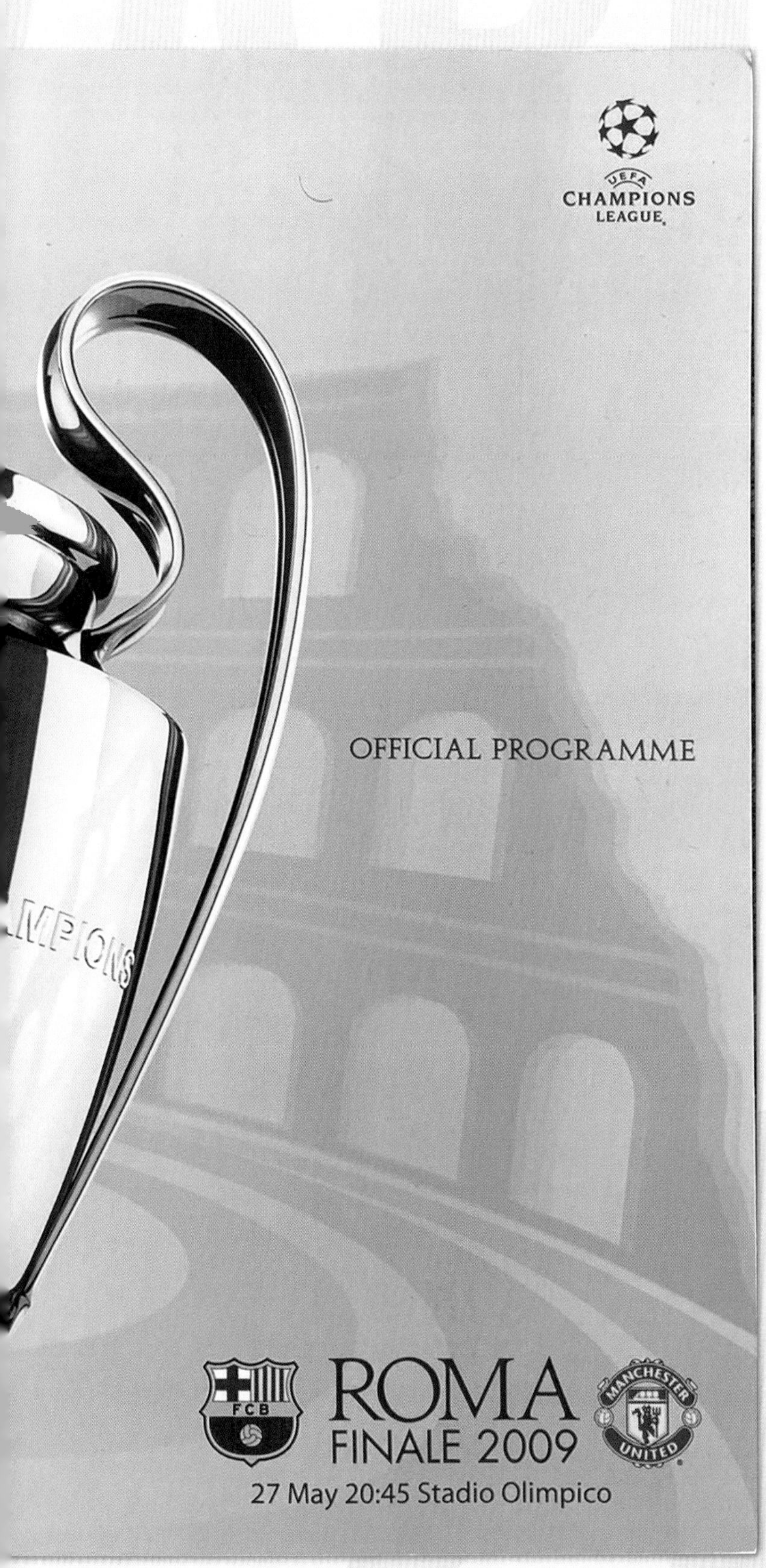
UEFA
CHAMPIONS
LEAGUE
OFFICIAL PROGRAMME
ROMA
FINALE 2009
27 May 20:45 Stadio Olimpico

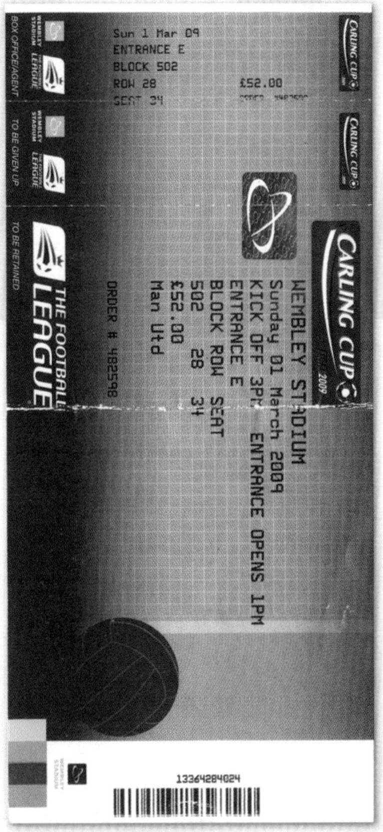
Sun 1 Mar 09
ENTRANCE E
BLOCK 502
ROW 28
SEAT 34
£52.00
CARLING CUP
WEMBLEY STADIUM
Sunday 01 March 2009
KICK OFF 3PM ENTRANCE OPENS 1PM
ENTRANCE E
BLOCK ROW SEAT
502 28 34
£52.00
Man Utd
ORDER # 482598
THE FOOTBALL LEAGUE
BOX OFFICE/AGENT
TO BE GIVEN UP
TO BE RETAINED
1336428402A

UEFA
CHAMPIONS
LEAGUE
ROMA FINALE 2009
TV
FOR SEATING PURPOSE ONLY
TRIBUNA
STAMPA
INFERIORE
39
3
SECTOR
COMMENTARY
POSITION
SEAT

CHAMPIONS BISTRO
WEDNESDAY
LUNCH
27 MAY 2009, 12:00 – 16:00
P
ROMA FINALE 2009

2011-

"A Remarkable Man" Bows Out

On the 2nd of September 2012, Ferguson celebrates his 1000th league game with United and his 100th game in the Champions League. He announces his retirement.

United burst upon the new season of 2010/11 with an extraordinary record; twenty-four games without defeat; until Wolverhampton Wanderers stopped them in their tracks 2-1 on February the 5th 2011.

Just one week later, the two Manchester teams were facing one another again and apart from the joy of beating the Blues 2-1 there was a magnificent goal from Wayne Rooney that Ferguson counts as the greatest goal in his time at United. With Nani's deflected cross sending the ball swinging into the City area from the right, Rooney rose unexpectedly to strike a pin-point accurate bicycle kick that put the ball in the back of the net. It truly was the achievement of a player with superb mind-body synthesis.

There had been a stinging 7-1 victory over Blackburn in November in which Berbatov was on fire scoring five, and an incisive 5-0 victory over Birmingham in January in which Berbatov was again deadly, scoring a hat-trick. This was particularly pleasing to both the manager and the player because the year before with just twelve goals to his credit, Berbatov – *"... he's a genius at times"*, according to the manager – had come in for a lot of criticism. As usual, when Ferguson believed in a player, not even the Black Riders could persuade the manager that it had been wrong to put his faith in him. Ferguson insisted that Berbatov had talent in abundance, *"good balance, composure on the ball and a fine scoring record"*. And, he said, he was athletic, tall and composed.

Neither could defeats at Chelsea and Liverpool put a brake on United's ascent towards their record-breaking nineteenth league title, which they took 9 points clear of Chelsea; 80 points to 71.

That all-important match against Chelsea in May when United were just three points clear of their rivals got off to a spectacular start when striker Javier Hernández hit the target after just one minute of play. United took off, whipped the ball around the Chelsea half and looked increasingly dangerous as they rattled the disorganised Chelsea defence. In the twenty-third minute Vidić put the home team two in front. Despite a goal by Chelsea twenty minutes from time, United continued to press forward and earn their deserved victory. Praise flowed thick and fast in the newspapers; *"... They possess a spirit too often missing in their main rivals... destroyed Chelsea on every level: technically and tacticall*

2013

" ... they have proved themselves players who rise to the occasion "

but also mentally".

United won their nineteenth title with one game to spare. It was Ferguson's twelfth league title. The Scot was understandably proud and exhilarated at being the manager of *"... the most successful team"*, the team that had finally knocked Liverpool off their perch.

And yet, there was a little doubt; were United any longer the razor-edged squad in every competition that had once made them feared at home and in Europe? When the question was raised, the manager answered evasively. *"... they have proved themselves players who rise to the occasion"* he was quoted in the Daily Mail. Yet outside of the League, something was preventing them from jumping the final hurdle. They were knocked out of the FA Cup challenge in the semi-final, a bitter defeat to their Manchester rivals, Manchester City, 0-1, and the League Cup challenge vanished in round five when they were well and truly smacked down by West Ham United, 4-0. There was hope when they topped their group in the Champions League and when they decisively beat both Chelsea, 1-0 and 2-1, and the German Side Schalka 04, 2-0 and 4-1, to earn a place in the final against Barcelona. Chelsea manager Carlo Ancelotti said later, *"Sir Alex is one of the greatest managers in the world ever, if not the greatest".*

Praise indeed for the manager of a team that caused Ancelotti to lose his job. But when it came to the crunch, Rooney's single goal in the final against Barcelona's three put the difference into perspective. United's team was impressive; Edwin van der Sar, Fabio, Ferdinand, Vidić and Evra, Giggs, Park, Carrick and Valencia guarding midfield with Hernandez and Rooney at the front. It has been described as one of the most talented sides ever assembled. The team prepared well, so well that the manager described it as the best he had ever seen.

United had sprung into action immediately and for the first ten minutes were playing in the Barcelona half. After fifteen minutes of this, Barcelona with the incomparable Lionel Messi, began to take back possession of the game. It was United's inability to deal adequately with Messi that Ferguson pinpointed as one of the failures of the team that night. And Wayne Rooney disappointed, unable to fulfill his role of penetrating the spaces behind the fullbacks. United were simply not up to par.

And when Barcelona resumed their ascendancy in the second half, it was Lionel Messi who did the damage with a second goal.

In talking about individual performances that night, the manager later came close to saying what many had long thought, that Berbatov, left out of the squad that night, had not turned out to be the player that Ferguson had hoped.

The Scot made another of his rare confessions about his fallibility after the game. Focused he said, on winning, he had urged Rooney to continue his role of attempting penetration behind the fullbacks, instead of redeploying players in different positions, remembering only afterwards that Barcelona won many of their games in the first fifteen minutes of the second half.

Even Ferguson confessed that Barcelona *"... mesmerise you with their passing"*, and that his team simply wasn't good enough on the night.

As a result of that deflating failure, Ferguson, with Scholes, a man whose opinions Fergie valued highly, and Neville, both of whom he employed as roving observers in the youth team, reserves and academy to assess the progress

Rooney competes with Branislav Ivanovic of Chelsea during their Premier League match at Old Trafford, 8th May 2011

Nani scores past Joe Hart of Manchester City during the FA Community Shield match at Wembley Stadium, 7th August 2011

> *" The manager is a genius and it is his belief and support that convinced me to stay "*

of players, began to reconsider how they were managing the youngsters and bringing them on from the Academy. Soon after, the average age of the squad was back down to twenty-four.

The season could have been worse still; there had been consternation and dismay in autumn 2010 when Rooney had put the knife in by saying that he wanted to leave the club, a statement that completely baffled Ferguson, who couldn't understand why anyone would want to leave what was one of the most successful clubs in British football. He had no idea, he said, what it was about. *"We can speculate... it won't matter a dickie bird, simply because the player Is adamant he wants to leave"*.

Perhaps one of the few moments when Ferguson's understanding of a player's motivation failed him. Perhaps he took it as a personal affront and hurt pride got in the way. Nonetheless, he took a softly-softly attitude, and was prepared to go the extra mile as he always was for players of exceptional talent, and he regarded Rooney as one of those. In this case, the extra mile meant more money, although Rooney padded quietly around the subject throwing up smokescreens with statements about *"vision"* and the squad not being strong enough; then there were gushes of mutual praise and admiration from all sides. Once more money was offered to Rooney, all the problems magically vanished and manager and player declared on the 22nd of October that Rooney was going nowhere because he had signed a new five-year contract. *"I'm pleased he has accepted the challenge to guide the younger players and establish himself as one of United's great players". That was the manager. "The manager is a genius and it is his belief and support that convinced me to stay".* That was the player.

Everyone saved face and United got back to the job in hand. Rooney seemed to have taken the incident to heart and knuckled down to deserving that support and belief from manager and fans.

Ferguson would probably have wished for a better season to have celebrated overtaking Sir Matt Busby's record of management on December the 19th 2010. An extraordinary achievement.

Something was slipping in the well-oiled Manchester United machine and that became very apparent in the following season, 2011/12. Apart from winning the Community Shield in August 2011, a satisfying 3-2 win against the other Manchester lads, there was nothing to show for the team's exertions that season.

At the far end of the season, the *"noisy neighbours"*, as Ferguson had once described them, Manchester City, would have the last laugh because they took the Premiership on goal difference from United when both teams topped the table with eighty-nine points each.

City took a horrible revenge on United just two months after the Community Shield defeat, completely overwhelming the Red Devils in a 6-1 victory at Old Trafford, the one hundred and sixtieth derby encounter.

Yet United had started out looking sharp even though they failed to create any chances of note. For the first twenty-two minutes everyone could have been forgiven for not foreseeing what was going to happen next.

It was the Blues who scored first. When half-time arrived there was still only one goal in it. Then catastrophe announced its presence when Jonny Evans was given his marching orders for holding back Balotelli. Balotelli had his revenge by scoring the second, and it didn't take too

> *"We live in a terrible, cynical world now, and when you lose a few games, the judge is out"*

long before the United defence had conceded the third. By this time the defence looked as though it might crumble completely.

Ferguson brought on Phil Jones, who couldn't resist the temptation to keep going forward. Then United's Darren Fletcher scored ten minutes from time and the United players decided to go for broke. Possibly the worst thing they could have done, and it added to the eventual goal difference at the end of the season between themselves and City.

The gaps that were now left yawning at the back were easily exploited by City, who whacked in another three in injury time alone. Fans were flown between excitement, thinking after the first United goal that a thrilling United comeback was around the corner, to despair at the 6-1 final scoreline. *"It looked humiliating but it was actually self annihilation"*. That was the manager's opinion. Ferguson felt that the opposition should never have been able to dissect United in that fashion.

No one had scored six goals against United in fifteen years, since Southampton in October 1996. Ferguson was crushed. *"I can't believe it, it is our worst day ever. It is the worst result in my history ever"*.

The manager, who was always considered to be a dictator and who readily confessed that he had a terrible temper, writes in his autobiography that after the game he *"... informed the players they had disgraced themselves". The game had been a farce in his eyes and he considered that after hammering City for forty minutes, the scoreline should have been the reverse of what it was. Having "informed"*, as he euphemistically described it, the team of his opinion, Ferguson set about stabilising his defensive lineup, which was where he detected weaknesses.

There was defeat at the hands of the Blues again later in the season, thankfully only 1-0 this time. It was more than enough.

Despite an unbeaten run of twelve games, United proved inconsistent at the wrong moments. When they lost 1-0 to Wigan, for example, the team they had thrashed 5-0 earlier in the season, a defeat that cost them the Premiership. They were also capable of putting five past Bolton, Fulham, and Wolverhampton, not to mention the trifling win against Arsenal when they rifled in a sensational eight goals to the London club's two.

That was a score that no one could have expected even twenty-two minutes into the game, which was when Welbeck scored United's first goal. A missed Arsenal penalty just a few minutes later gave an indication that bottom of the table Arsenal were still in with a chance.

That mistaken perception was soon put to bed when Young curled in the second on twenty-eight minutes and the floodgates opened. Rooney, causing all kinds of chaos in the Arsenal defence, scored three, and Nani and Park all added to Arsenal's woes before Young sent the ball looping into the Arsenal net from his right foot for the final goal in the first minute of injury time.

Ferguson, aware of the vagaries of the game and that Arsène Wenger's woes today might well be his tomorrow, including calls for his head on a stake, expressed sympathy for the Arsenal manager.

"We live in a terrible, cynical world now, and when you lose a few games, the judge is out and you see managers going early in the season many, many times over".

José Mourinho was to feel the steel sting of this immutable rule in the 2015/16 season, when the Premiership-

Danny Welbeck watches the ball as he's closed down by Laurent Koscielny of Arsenal during the Barclays Premier League match at Old Trafford, 28th August 2011

winning manager of the summer was fired before the year was out.

Ferguson mentioned that his team could have scored even more goals, but that *"... you don't want to score more against a weakened team like that"*. An odd remark, perhaps. Maybe he simply meant that chances were missed that should have been taken; because, as in this season, goal difference can usher in glory or gloom.

Snakes and ladders, then; sadly there were more snakes.

Whilst the League battle was intense – United were on top with three games left to play – elsewhere there was nothing to take home but bitter disappointment. The League Cup challenge had collapsed on the 30th of November when Crystal Palace pushed them out, 2-1. In January 2012, Liverpool, of all teams, nudged them out of the FA Cup by the

“ will United take a record twentieth league title? ”

same margin, after United had shoved Manchester City off the board in round three, 3-2. For only the third time in seventeen years, United failed to progress past the group stage of the Champions League, finishing third in the table behind Benfica and Basel.

As third in the table they entered the Europa League and after just scraping past Ajax with one win and one loss, they were then toppled by Athletic Bilbao, 2-3 and 2-1. Alex Ferguson was later heavily criticised for describing the Europa League as a *“punishment”*. He apologised later, but for a man used to the status accorded by the major competitions, the Europa League was second best, and he truly felt that playing in it was punishment for losing. United had failed to reach a cup final for the first time in over ten years.

All in all, a dismal outing for a side used to huge success.

What had gone wrong?

There seemed to be a great consensus amongst the fans that United were missing a world-class defensive midfielder. Many were also of the opinion that Michael Owen was not the player he used to be and that despite Wayne Rooney’s impressive haul of goals, 34 in total, some of his former magic was also lacking.

“Apparent complacency in approach and gross underestimation of the opponents” was one criticism of the side’s lack of achievement in Europe. There were injuries, of course; United would not be the first team to be plagued by those; Darren Fletcher, Anderson and Tom Cleverly were absent for large stretches of time and Vidić was out of the side for almost three months; his superb leadership and playing skills were sorely missed.

As he shuffled his severely diminished team, Ferguson’s experience as a manager paid off when Evans, Ryan Giggs, Michael Carrick, Paul Scholes (back from retirement) and co., almost pulled off the title race. Under analysis, it seemed that this was hardly the prelude to the end of the Red Empire that some were predicting. Still, Fergie was getting on in years, and it was undeniable that those big cup-winning seasons were beginning to recede into the distance; so it was understandable that questions began to arise about Ferguson’s future at the club.

By the middle of November 2012, however, when United were back in first place, those questions were secondary to *“will United take a record twentieth league title?”*.

The signs were good; all the big challengers, Manchester City, Chelsea and Arsenal, had all been beaten before the year was out. Those were all close-run matches, with Chelsea and Manchester City forcing the Reds to score three to beat them, 3-2 each time, whilst Arsenal went down 2-1.

Ferguson made no bones about the fact that the match against City had been important, not only because a win would give them a six-point lead at the top of the table, but also because there were strong emotions involved; it would make up for losing the title to them in the previous season. *“I will never forget how I felt that night after we had lost it and that will give us more motivation, definitely”*, was Ferguson’s opinion.

There was tension in the air, obviously, from the start with City gaining the upper hand whilst United absorbed the pressure with their 4-4-1-1 line up.

In the sixteenth minute United broke forward and Rooney was there to put United in the lead. City conceded a second in the twenty-ninth minute after they had lost their captain through injury. Again, it was Rooney who did the damage with his one hundred and fiftieth goal for the club. After a disallowed United goal, City pulled out the stops as the

Sir Alex walks off at halftime during the Barclays Premier League match against Swansea City at Old Trafford, 6th May 2012

excitement built, and a low shot by Yaya Touré gave them their first goal.

There followed some exciting football and close calls for both teams. City were now giving United a run for their money and with only four minutes left to play, the ball found its way back into the United net. 2-2.

Ironically, it was former United player Tevez who, by fouling Rafael and giving away a free kick, enabled United to score their third goal. United had their revenge even though they had tested their fans' nervous systems to the utmost yet again.

The manager, naturally, was delighted with the result in a game about which he said, *"You could not take your eyes off it. It was such an engrossing game"*. It was a great day for the club, he went on, *"... to get six points clear and beat our closest rivals"*.

Revenge is, indeed, sweet.

Chelsea's revenge was to beat United 1-0 later in the year and knock them out of the FA Cup challenge in the sixth round by the same score. This defeat hurt all the more because Chelsea had also knocked them out of the League Cup competition, 4-5, in October 2012.

The United challenge in the Champions League started strongly with four back-to-back victories. Galatasaray, CFR Cluj and Braga went down before the red wave.

And then the cracks began to appear.

Defeat by Galatasaray, CFR Cluj was not tragic and they still emerged top of their group. But when they came up against Real Madrid, they simply lacked the power to overcome the Spaniards, drawing their first match 1-1 and losing at home in the second leg 1-2. It was bitter that Cristiano Ronaldo had scored in both matches for the Spanish side.

In the Premiership, United continued to power towards the title with an eighteen-match undefeated run that only Manchester City put an end to, 2-1 at home, on the 8th of April 2013. It couldn't reverse United's dominance of the table, however, no more than the defeat against Chelsea.

The last game of the season would have no bearing on Manchester United's place at the top of the table. It turned out to be again filled with emotional content, because on the 8th of May, Sir Alex Ferguson had announced his intention to retire at the end of the season. Rumour had got there first, of course, leaving an uneasy sensation in fan's stomachs. It was a shock when it happened, nonetheless.

Now there was obviously a danger that this final match would turn out to be nothing more than a showcase, with United players wanting to send their manager off with a final victory. What the teams produced was indeed a showcase but not as anyone could have imagined it; the match turned into a thrilling game of attacking football.

West Bromwich Albion certainly had no intention of being the fall guys in this scenario. But six minutes into the game, it looked as though that was what was going to happen when a forty-yard pass from Hernandez found the head of Kagawa and United were in front. Three minutes later it seemed as though a massacre was unfolding as the ball deflected from Olsson for the second goal.

West Bromwich were having none of that, however, and managed to keep out a swarming United team until the thirtieth minute. This time it was Büttner who swept a low drive into the net. Again the Baggies fought back and were

United's players celebrate Robin Van Persie's late winner as City fans throw coins and a smoke bomb onto the pitch during the Premier League match against Manchester City at The Etihad stadium, 9th December 2012

rewarded with a goal just before half-time by Morrison. 3-1 when the teams left the field.

West Brom brought on Lukaka for the second half and suddenly his team were invested with new life. The substitute pushed in the second for West Brom and put United's win in danger. It was Robin van Persie who seemed to have put the game out of reach of the home team when he clinched United's fourth in the fifty-third minute and Hernandez put in what was surely the deathblow ten minutes later.

Paul Scholes then made his final appearance for the Red Devils, earning himself a yellow card for the privilege. And then Lukaka was in front of goal again ten minutes before the end to put in his second goal.

Not to be outdone, Mulumba added number four. Lukaka replied to that insolence by getting his hat-trick. The score was a magnificent 5-5.

And that is how it ended.

Ferguson might have wished that his team had not

Ryan Giggs takes on Claudio Yacob (L) and Youssuf Mulumbu of West Brom during their Barclays Premier League match at The Hawthorns, 19th May 2013

given away a three-goal lead twice in one game. But it was all out of his hands now. He walked onto the pitch, hands above his head, acknowledging the faithful United fans. The moment United supporters never wanted to experience had now arrived; Alex Ferguson walked from the pitch down into the tunnel away from the adulation of the crowds and his managerial career. An extraordinary career was over.

For a record twentieth time, United were league champions, with 89, a dominating 11 points clear of second-placed Manchester City on 78 points.

There was a celebration, but it was also tinged with a sense of the greatest sadness. Ferguson was seventy-one, which made him the oldest-serving manager in the League at the time. Twenty-six years as manager were over. That made him the longest-serving manager in England. In that time, he had won twenty-five major trophies, thirty-eight in all, another managerial record and one that is unlikely ever to be broken. As the former footballer and current England manager Roy Hodgson said on hearing the news of Ferguson's retirement, *"No one will be able to match his achievements, his dedication, his support for colleagues in need, and his team-building know-how"*.

" No one will be able to match his achievements... "

"The only way you can keep your job is by being successful", Ferguson wrote later. *"It's a results industry, and managers lose their job if they lose two or three games in a row, sometimes only one game. It's an absolute intense industry in that you have to be successful... You have moments where you have bad spells, but I'm pretty good with dealing with defeat. I usually get better"*.

He wasn't going to leave the club, but stay in the background as a director and ambassador, so his experience would not be lost.

What did the great man himself have to say at the end? There were no interviews after the match and just three words when asked how he felt; *"Emotional, very emotional"*.

The thoughts on his career he wrote down after he had retired. Success was not all down to the manager, he knew that, of course. *"... in developing a team with United, you have to develop the character of the dressing room, you have to have people in whom I sometimes like to see myself"*. There were he said, men in the club with character and that enabled them to win titles; they would not accept defeat.

Sir Alex Ferguson is given a 'guard of honour' prior to his 1,500th and final match in charge of the club ahead of the Barclays Premier League match against West Bromwich Albion at The Hawthorns, 19th May 2013

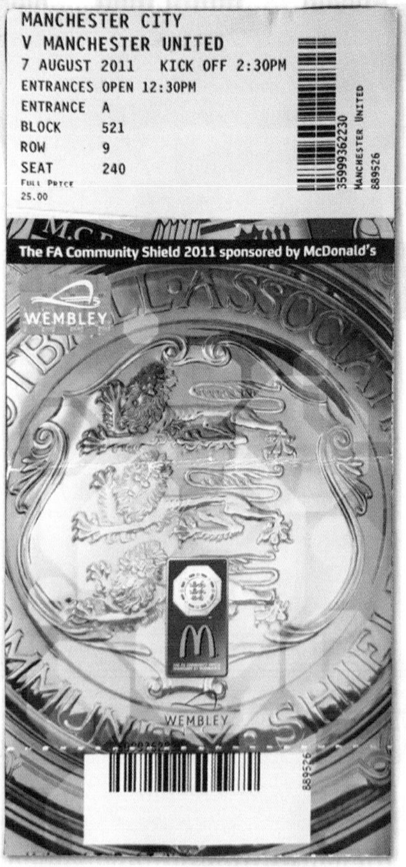
MANCHESTER CITY
V MANCHESTER UNITED
7 AUGUST 2011 KICK OFF 2:30PM
ENTRANCES OPEN 12:30PM
ENTRANCE A
BLOCK 521
ROW 9
SEAT 240
FULL PRICE
25.00
35999362230
MANCHESTER UNITED
889526
The FA Community Shield 2011 sponsored by McDonald's
WEMBLEY
WEMBLEY
889526

M.C.F.C.
The FA Community Shield 2011 sponsored by McDonald's
MANCHESTER CITY v MANCHESTER UNITED
SUNDAY 7 AUGUST 2011, 2.30PM
OFFICIAL MATCHDAY PROGRAMME
WEMBLEY STADIUM £5
COMMUNITY · SHIE

MANCHESTER UNITED
CHAMP19NS
United Review
Official matchday programme £3
2011/12 Season Volume 73 Issue 2
v Arsenal 28.08.11
4pm
Inside today's issue
• Tom Cleverley interview
• Our rivals: the lowdown
• Nicky Butt's favourite game
• Title years: 1911
SIR ALEX FERGUSON ON THE NEXT GENERATION
"WE STILL BELIEVE IN YOUNG PLAYERS: THAT'S WHAT THIS CLUB IS ABOUT"
WELBECK
19
BARCLAYS PREMIER LEAGUE

A Change of Pace.

Retirement did not mean that Sir Alex was going to sit quietly and simply exchange football boots for carpet slippers as the plaudits continued to flow in. In 2017, he was acclaimed as one of the 10 most influential coaches since the foundation of UEFA in 1954. His interest in life was too great for that static scenario. But he did take a break from everything the year he retired, relaxing on a well-earned cruise up the islands in Scotland with his family.

Sir Alex's passion for horse racing has been well-documented, and he was still at the pinnacle of his achievements at Old Trafford when he concluded that getting involved in horse racing might be helpful in ironing out a few of the stresses and strains of football management. Investing some £17,000 in two-year-old Queensland Star – he named the horse in honour of a ship his father had helped build in the Govan shipyard – he sent his new acquisition out to run on the flat at Newmarket in April 1998. Queensland Star came home first.

In buying a racehorse, Ferguson was proving that he was a chip off the old block, as his dad used to place his "tanner Yankee" bet each Saturday on the horses. (A tanner was a colloquial name for sixpence, and a Yankee is 11 bets of equal value placed on selections in four separate events.)

In April 2021, at a Grand National meeting, Sir Alex enjoyed what he termed was his "best day" at a racecourse. That was quite a claim, because he has owned horses for over 20years, and one of them, Rock of Gibraltar, had seven wins on the flat in Group One races and won twice in the Boxing Day meetings in the King George VI Chase at Kempton Park.

His April 2021 winners were Protektorat, Monmiral and Clan Des Obeaux, who all crossed the line to bring their owner a Grade One treble.

Sir Alex is not only a racehorse owner but also a generous donor to many charities, and his interest in horse racing also feeds that side of his life. One racehorse he owned, which had also charged to victory in many races, was the thoroughbred *I'm Fraam Govan* - generally known as 'Guv'. As the horse came to the end of its racing career, Ferguson decided to donate the champion to the Pastures New charity which has stables in Littleborough, Rochdale. Ferguson – along with Paul Scholes – is a patron of the charity created in 2012, which retrains and finds new homes for racehorses that have been retired or injured.

Another of his interests that predates his retirement is collecting wines as an investment. Over the years, he acquired a seriously expensive collection, buying Pétrus, Domaine de la Romanée-Conti, Lynch-Bages and Lafite Rothschild. Every year since 1996, he has bought a selection from Château Pétrus in Bordeaux and from the Domaine de la Romanée-Conti in Burgundy, which produces some of the best and most expensive wines in the world.

Yet, he recalls his earlier life with Cathy when he bought a bottle of wine costing £15 for his wedding anniversary. *"I brought it home and my wife Cathy said: "How much did you pay for that?" I said, £15. "Fifteen pounds!", she said, "Are you off your head?"*

It would seem that his head was very firmly on his shoulders, however, when in 2014 he auctioned part of his collection, which brought in over £2.2 million. *"In retirement"*, he's quoted as saying, *"I now have the time to visit the places*

" ... If you want to do well in life, you've got to sacrifice"

and people that will feed my passion, so I felt it made sense to release a large number of the wines I had collected over the years. I hope many will enjoy exploring my collection".

Wine collecting, like racing, had begun as a distraction from the trials and tribulations of football life, a break that allowed him to rebalance and recover from the "*intensity and demands required of me as the manager of Manchester United*".

Sir Alex continued learning all through his illustrious career, of course, and education is still a very important subject for the former manager. He was made an honorary graduate of Glasgow Caledonian University to which he has donated £500,000. GCU launched its Foundation with the donation, and The Sir Alex Ferguson Scholarship and Awards Fund now delivers scholarship programmes and awards for students from all walks of life and across all disciplines. Many students benefit from his generosity, which fosters greater participation by funding mobility and travel awards.

And, of course, sport is always in the forefront of his mind. Not only does he carry out an ambassadorial role at Manchester United, his childhood team Harmony Row are pleased that he is a long-term patron for them.

Children and youngsters have always been an integral part of Sir Alex's life, as he proved when he first arrived at Manchester United and immediately set about upgrading the importance of bringing young players into the team. In that spirit, he is also a sporting ambassador for another charity, Street Child United.

In the intervening years since his retirement, Sir Alex has often spoken about his long and now legendary career with Manchester United and his outlook on life and leadership. He is, in fact, a sought-after speaker on the latter subject. Harvard Business School were so impressed by his management skills that in 2013, immediately after he had retired, they asked him to teach at the school, where he subsequently gave lecture s on leadership to some of the most powerful executives in the world. Quite an acknowledgement of his abilities.

One of his main tenets at Manchester was to clear the air as soon as possible, which ran against the grain of the man and friend he admired immensely, a man who was a legend in his own right, former Celtic manager Jock Stein. "*I always believe I should address matters straight after the game*", said Ferguson, "*He always said it was better to leave it to the Monday when everyone had calmed down a bit*". That was fine for most people, added Sir Alex. But Sir Alex was not most people. "*... that was not my nature. My nature was to get it all out the road and start afresh the next day.*"

In retrospect, Sir Alex once mused, he realised that he had sacrificed most of his life in return for the extraordinary success he had achieved at Manchester. In one interview, he commented: "But you know, to achieve that type of success, the word sacrifice comes about all the time. If you want to do well in life, you've got to sacrifice".

Working with such utter dedication whilst maintaining a healthy marriage was only possible because he knew that he could rely "100 per cent" on his wife Cathy, who, he gladly acknowledged, had selflessly brought up their children and run his domestic life so that he could concentrate on his career. In a rare glimpse into his emotional life, Sir Alex said, "*Words are not enough to express what this has meant to me*".

But he had also tempered his dedication, and he cautioned that it could not come with the price tag of totally ignoring, abusing, or even forgetting about family life. In his own words: "*... you need to have a drive and an energy and a personality that can deal with all the various things attached to having a family and also managing a football team*".

In the years following his retirement, more information came to light about the manager's reasons for leaving Manchester. The experience was, as he put it, "*pretty strange*". And the final game, as might be expected, was not easy. When asked about it, he conceded that he'd had a few days when he was "*wobblin' a bit*", adding, however, true to his life's philosophy, "*But you just have to gather yourself*".

Having made the decision to leave Manchester United the previous Christmas, he was not the kind of person to ever look back. "*The decision to retire is one that I have thought a great deal about. It is the right time*", he told the BBC. However, his wife's twin sister, Bridget, had only recently passed away, and as the manager told his players: "*I feel that I owe it to my wife to be with her and look after her. It's been unbelievable and thanks for everything, I've loved every minute... I don't really want to go, but I've got to take this decision*".

Sir Alex expressed doubts that in the present era of football he would ever be able to approach management in the same way that he had done when he started at Manchester, from the roots up. "*Now it's three losses and you're out*", he mused, an attitude that left no time for concentrating on anything but the immediate future. He also revealed that having left the club in what he felt was a good condition to face future challenges, "*...I'm not being critical, but when I saw some of my players actually leaving the club, I didn't quite enjoy that, you know, as in: Why? ... I mean, these guys have won the league by 11 points. Give them another year. That was hard to accept*".

Nonetheless, he was wise enough to know that he should let go and he did. From that point on, he said, he no longer needed to think about what he would have done. That part of his life was over. A new one had begun, one in which he could simply relax with a glass of wine beforehand, and then sit back and enjoy the games.

Relating one anecdote from his early years in football, Sir Alex also spoke about the time when he was a young player at St. Johnstone and found himself being arrested for getting involved in a drunken brawl. Not something the later Sir Alex would have approved of. In court, he was handed a fine of £3 for assault. The cause was his upset at not being included in the Scottish club's first team, which had made him take to drink and subsequently to lose control of his behaviour. One immediate effect of that behaviour was that his family stamped him as a 'black sheep', and Ferguson and his father didn't speak to one another for two years.

Being in control at all times was another principle that Sir Alex set great store by. Which is why the after-effects of the most frightening event of his life were so alien and unwelcome for him.

In 2018, Manchester United FC issued a statement concerning their former manager: "Sir Alex Ferguson has undergone emergency surgery today for a brain haemorrhage. The procedure has gone very well, but he needs a period of intensive care to optimise his recovery. His family request privacy in this matter".

It was the 5th of May.

On the day it happened, Ferguson's son Jason recalled phoning United's club doctor and asking him two questions to which the doctor replied immediately, "*Look, I think he's had a bleed in the brain. You really need an ambulance now*".

Ferguson spent several days in intensive care following the operation, doctors giving him just a 20% chance of survival. As he lay alone in his hospital bed, Sir Alex remembers that he felt lost. "*I mean, when I woke up hours later after the operation. You feel loneliness*". Then he wondered: "*Am I going to be alright? You know, because just two days ago I was fit as a fiddle, playing a game of golf sometimes, on the bike and exercising, you never anticipate it was going to happen like that*". It all left him with a sense of isolation. "*I did feel vulnerable.*"

It was his memory that caused him the greatest concern, fear of losing his memory upon which he had always been able to depend, often scorning other managers who would carry notebooks around with them. He recalled the moment when he thought it was happening: *"... my two grandsons were in with me, and all of a sudden I stopped talking, I just couldn't get a word out... at that moment I was a bit terrified to be honest with you"*.

What was he going to do, he wondered, if he couldn't talk and his memory had failed him? Once his speech therapist got to work on him, however, he worked as hard as ever on getting himself back to health. He praised her highly, mentioning how she had made him write down his family's names and his players' names. In just over one week, his memory had returned.

"All of my life I have appreciated the NHS", he said afterwards, *"None more so than with that experience, they were fantastic. And I owe it to them, really"*.

The terrible experience changed him as a person and made him aware of his vulnerability. But he also came to accept that vulnerability and therefore not take life too seriously. *"... if I go tomorrow I'll be grateful for three years extra I had. That's a feeling I've had for quite a while now"*.

Acceptance was not easy. But he had never shirked from making really difficult decisions in life – and this acceptance was one of those decisions. Admitting that he was no longer in control of his health was not a condition he could easily live with as he had always been in control at United and expected his players to understand and accept that fact. But accept it he did, confirming that he had done so by mentioning that, of course, it had been a long journey, *"... but I'm making steps forward, doing what my son tells me and what the doctors tell me, so It's really good"*.

Ferguson showed his gratitude for the life-saving surgery and care he'd been given, by raising over £400,000 at a gala dinner for Salford Royal Hospital, where he had undergone his emergency brain surgery. It was, he said, a thank you to the NHS for the care he had received.

More recently, Ferguson lent his support to Manchester United and England player, Marcus Rashford in his FairShare campaign to have free school meals provided during holiday periods for low-income families in England, as well as other supporting measures.

Ferguson was 100 per cent behind the young player's actions and called him on the phone right away: *"I thought what he was doing is an example for a young person to give to all the rest of them in this industry... I was so proud of him, I really was... he's not got carried away with himself. He's still trying to do an honest job as you would expect from him"*. Sir Alex pointed out that becoming rich and famous can often become a problem, a burden that some can carry better than others. He had seen it happen and knew better than many how stardom and money can change people. Rashford's campaign prompted major changes in government policy.

In one interview he gave at the time, the former Manchester United manager allowed a glimpse into one of the driving aspects of his attitude to all that he has done. "You can't forget your upbringing because that's what made me". Together with British philanthropist Sir Michael Moritz – he and Ferguson are friends – Ferguson agreed to match every donation made to the FareShare programme that Marcus Rashford was promoting in his attempts to prevent children from going hungry and for which he received high praise.

Sir Alex bravely allowed his son Jason to produce a documentary about his life, called 'Sir Alex Ferguson: Never Give In', which was premiered in 2021. Consistent with his reputation for honesty and straightforward communication, the former manager did not shrink from speaking about the more difficult moments of his life. *"He knows me better than anyone. And I was happy to go ahead with it"*, he said when asked about how he felt about Jason being in charge of the documentary.

Sir Alex also entered the fierce debate that erupted when it was disclosed that major European football clubs, including Manchester United, were intending to form a breakaway Super

League in 2021. He said that the idea of a European Super League would be a departure from 70 years of football history. *"Fans all over love the competition as it is... in my time at United, we played in four Champions League finals, and they were always the most special of nights."*

Sir Alex no doubt approved of the result of the outrage that followed the announcement; the clubs backed down. The Premier League was left intact for another season.

Measured but forceful and fearless intervention sums up very well the character of the man who spearheaded the Manchester United charge through those extraordinary years; years blessed with transcendent performances by players of thrilling ability guided by a confident and intelligent mind. Triumphs and huge disappointments had paraded before the fans' delighted, disappointed and often tear-filled eyes in over a quarter of a century of unparalleled entertainment under the superlative leadership of a uniquely gifted manager.

Sir Alex Ferguson.

THE STATISTICS:

LEAGUE POSITIONS.

English League Div One

1986/87 - 11

1987/88 - 2

1988/89 - 11

1989/90 - 13

1990/91 - 6

1991/92 - 2

English Premier League

1992/93 - 1

1993/94 - 1

1994/95 - 2

1995/96 - 1

1996/97 - 1

1997/98 - 2

1998/99 - 1

1999/2000 - 1

2000/01 - 1

2001/02 - 3

2002/03 - 1

2003/04 - 3

2004/05 - 3

2005/06 - 2

2006/07 - 1

2007/08 - 1

2008/09 - 1

2009/10 - 2

2010/11 - 1

2011/12 - 2

2012/13 - 1

MANCHESTER UNITED TITLES & AWARDS WITH ALEX FERGUSON:

Premier League:
1992-93, 1993-94, 1995-96, 1996-97, 1998-99, 1999-2000, 2000-01, 2002-03, 2006-07, 2007-08, 2008-09, 2010-11, 2012-13

FA Cup:
1989-90, 1993-94, 1995-96, 1998-99, 2003-04

League Cup:
1991-92, 2005-06, 2008-09, 2009-10

FA Charity/Community Shield:
1990 (shared), 1993, 1994, 1996, 1997, 2003, 2007, 2008, 2010, 2011

UEFA Champions League:
1998-99, 2007-08

UEFA Cup Winners' Cup:
1990-91

UEFA Super Cup:
1991

Intercontinental Cup:
1999

FIFA Club World Cup:
2008

ALEX FERGUSON INDIVIDUAL AWARDS:

Premier League Manager of the Season:
1993-94, 1995-96, 1996-97, 1998-99, 1999-2000, 2002-03, 2006-07, 2007-08, 2008-09, 2010-11, 2012-13

Premier League Manager of the Month:
August 1993, October 1994, February 1996, March 1996, February 1997, October 1997, January 1999, April 1999,August 1999, March 2000, April 2000, February 2001, April 2003, December 2003, February 2005, March 2006, August 2006, October 2006, February 2007,January 2008, March 2008, January 2009, April 2009, September 2009, January 2011, August 2011, October 2012

LMA Manager of the Decade:
1990s

LMA Manager of the Year:
1998-99, 2007-08, 2010-11, 2012-13

LMA Special Merit Award:
2009, 2011

UEFA Manager of the Year:
1998-99

UEFA Team of the Year:
2007, 2008

Onze d'Or Coach of the Year:
1999, 2007, 2008

IFFHS World's Best Club Coach:
1999, 2008

World Soccer Magazine World Manager of the Year:
1993, 1999, 2007, 2008

BBC Sports Personality of the Year Coach Award:
1999

BBC Sports Personality Team of the Year Award:
1999

Laureus World Sports Award for Team of the Year:
2000

BBC Sports Personality of the Year Lifetime Achievement Award:
2001

English Football Hall of Fame (as manager):
2002

Scottish Football Hall of Fame:
2004

European Hall of Fame (as manager):
2008

FIFA Presidential Award:
2011

Premier League 10 Seasons Awards:
1992-93 to 2001-02

Premier League 20 Seasons Awards:
1992-93 to 2011-12

IFFHS World's Best Coach of the 21st Century:
2012

Most Coaching Appearances:
392 matches

FWA Tribute Award:
1996

Mussabini Medal:
1999

PFA Merit Award:
2007

Premier League Merit Award:
2012-13

BBC Sports Personality Diamond Award:
2013

Northwest Football Awards:
2013

IFFHS All Time World's Best Coach
1996-2020

France Football, 2nd Greatest Manager of All Time
2019

FourFourTwo, Greatest Manager of All Time
2020

OTHER PERSONAL AWARDS:

OBE: Officer of the Order of the British Empire:
1983

CBE: Commander of the Order of the British Empire:
1995

Knight Bachelor (Kt.):
1999

Freedom of the City of Aberdeen:
1999

Freedom of the City of Glasgow:
1999

Freedom of the City of Manchester:
2000

Freedom of the Borough of Trafford:
2013

A FEW SIR ALEX FERGUSON QUOTES.

"It's getting tickly now - squeaky-bum time, I call it." (Referring to the 2003 title race.)

"When I think of disappointments, obviously Jaap Stam was always a disappointment to me, I made a bad decision there."

"I never concentrated on how many games I'd won".

"...your trust and loyalty and your personality. These are without question the characteristics you really need. Communication is so vital."

"Working hard is a real talent."

"... as a manager I never looked back. I always looked to the next day."

"Management is based on communication loyalty and trust... communication was really important to me, recognising value in my staff."

"Bobby Charlton, in particular, was a great supporter of what I was trying to achieve."

"But it would help if his greetings were accompanied by a decent glass of wine. What he gave me was paint-stripper." (Referring to José Mourinho.)

"When I was 21, I went for my badges, my coaching badges. And I got them by the time I was 26. And I kept going back to the coaching schools every year; I prepared myself to be a manager."

"I was always concentrating on winning the next trophy. Move on, move on. And when you look at it now, I'll try to put the cups in place, in order. And I have to check it again. Because I never bothered with that. I only bother with the next game."

"Sometimes you look in a field and you see a cow and you think it's a better cow than the one you've got in your own field. It's a fact. Right? And it never really works out that way." (Following Wayne Rooney's transfer request in 2010.)

"Do you think I would enter into a contract with that mob? Absolutely no chance. I would not sell them a virus. That is a 'No', by the way. There is no agreement whatsoever between the clubs." (Referring to selling Cristiano Ronaldo to Real Madrid.)

"Deep down... I never expected to win a game ever."

"Have you ever scored from 25 yards Gary? (Gary Neville.) No. Then why the hell are you trying it here now!"

Besides his ambassadorial role for UNICEF UK, Sir Alex Ferguson also supports many other charities, including:

Barnado's
National Breast Cancer Foundation
National Literacy Trust
Nordoff Robbins
Oxfam
Shane Arne Foundation
Sir Bobby Robson Foundation
Sport Relief
UNICEF
Willow Foundation
Wounded Warrior Project